First Edition

A GUIDE FOR SUSTAINING CONVERSATIONS ON RACISM, IDENTITY, AND OUR MUTUAL HUMANITY

By Steve Burghardt, Kalima DeSuze, Linda Lausell Bryant, and Mohan Vinjamuri

Bassim Hamadeh, CEO and Publisher

Kassie Graves, Director of Acquisitions and Sales

Jamie Giganti, Senior Managing Editor

Jess Estrella, Senior Graphic Designer

Kassie Graves, Acquisitions Editor

Brian Fahey, Licensing Associate

Berenice Quirino, Associate Production Editor

Joyce Lue, Interior Designer

Printed in the United States of America.

ISBN: 978-1-5165-1989-7 (pbk) /978-1-5165-1990-3 (br)

Contents

PART ONE: BEFORE WE ENTER THE CLASSROOM
(Faculty Preparation)

"Before We Enter the Classroom" features a dialogue about the personal, community, and institutional infrastructure necessary to make these conversations authentic, sustainable, and meaningful.

PART TWO: THE CLASSROOM CONVERSATIONS
(Faculty-Student Conversations)

"The Classroom Conversations" features the hot-button questions, usually from students, that faculty have asked for support to further bolster their ability to appropriately respond in the classroom.

PART THREE: SHIFTING THE TEACHING PARADIGM

Keeping the Conversation Going: Reflections for a School's Faculty and Students
"Shifting the Teaching Paradigm" features lessons for critical pedagogy, classroom management, and learning.

Dedicated to

(S. B.): Liz Laboy & Evelyn Petersen—two women whose conversations have helped sustain me, especially when I didn't want to listen.

(K. D.): My community both near and far. Ninth, St., Colon y Tres, Veinte, Brooklyn—siempre.

(L. L.-B.): My husband Marshall, my children Jasmine, Sara, Gideon, Gabriel, Dyami, and Antoine, and all crusaders for social justice.

(M. V.): My students who have taught me and helped me grow as a human being.

Dedicated to

Acknowledgments

(S. B.): As the years go on, the thanks increase geometrically. I have to begin with my students who have taught me so much for so long. Feisty, not easily impressed, more concerned about social justice as it's lived and not simply taught, unafraid to challenge authority, occasionally going too far and crossing a line that turned out needed to be crossed, they inspire me far more than I could ever inspire them. It's no accident that my three co-authors first showed up in my classrooms over the years. Each taught me (and, yes, I hope I taught them, too) before they left to enter the world to make significant marks of commitment in as many communities as possible: child welfare, Dreamers, LGBTQ folks, anti-racism work. In retrospect, I realized that what united Kalima, Linda, and Mohan was not just their commitment to anti-racism work but their openness, vulnerability, and belief in the capacity of others, especially those with less power, to make our world a better place. And, of course, Elisabeth Rossi (who also ended up in one of my classrooms, already a co-teacher) and her artwork reveal very much the same. Finally, much gratitude to Lorraine Gutierrez, for taking the time from her ever-busy schedule to write such a thoughtful and compassionate Foreword.

So many others have added so much: long-time and new colleagues at Silberman School of Social Work, with special shout-outs to Terry Mizrahi for her friendship and collegiality over thirty-five years, Robyn Brown-Manning, Willie Tolliver, and Samuel Aymer, and all my other fellow Lab teachers for our work inside the Practice Lab with the Anti-Oppression Lens, where 'keepin' on keepin' on' was our daily shared commitment to this important work. My work on the Special Commission to Advance Macro Practice has given me the pleasure to get to know, respect, and enjoy the company of many professional colleagues, especially Darlyne Bailey, Michel Coconis, Mark Homan, Rebecca Sander, and Tracy Soska. Others in the world of child welfare made an equal impact on me due to their integrity and lifetime commitment to New York City's and our nation's most vulnerable children: Melissa baker, William Bell, Eric Brettschneider, Joe Cardieri, Gladys Carrion, Zeinab Chahine, William Fletcher, Dale Joseph, Jennifer Jones Austin, Jacqueline Martin, Jacqueline McKnight, Nigel Nathaniel, Susan Nuccio, Liz Roberts, Charita Thomas, Jess Dannhauser, Sharmeela

Mediratta, Kim Watson, Anne Williams-Isom, and Hillary Williams. The special team of people whom I worked alongside as a consultant over the years grew to be friends and trusted partners, as well: together, Ed Laboy, Robyn Hatcher, Linda Johnson, Bill McKeithan, "U-Bob" Perry, Jacqueline Snape, and Deborah Sanders, along with Liz Laboy and I, shared as much laughter as hard work—a pretty rare experience these days, especially as there were occasional tears, too.

Finally, a few other friends and family members who brought me joy. To begin: lifetime friends Mike Fabricant and Eric Zachary; my dear wife Pat Beresford, who manages to keep me in conversations that make me stronger, walks hand-in-hand with me through life's heartaches and happiness, and still dances better than anyone I know; the Beacon Bs, Lila, Matty, Desmond, and Simone, lovers of music, providing laughter over a good bottle of wine or beer (well, the kids have milk), and who remain committed to what is just and what is just fun; Josh, whose humor is matched by his smarts and warm heart; Eric and Lisa, each with humor both as dry as it is always on-point; and Jen and Sara, walk-in-the rain kinda gals who make me laugh and warm my heart—without all of them, life would be so very much less.

We all have deep appreciation for the entire Cognella team, beginning with my friend and publisher extraordinaire Kassie Graves, who helped create this book; our wonderful first copyeditor Lisa Bess Kramer, who gave us confidence that we might have something to offer others; and the entire Cognella team—Mike Augsdorfer, Jess Estrella, Jaime Giganti, Dani Skeen, Berenice Quirino, and Dave Wilson.

(K. D.): "I am because you are." When I was young, my brother would call me "Blacky," and I never took it as an insult. Whether that was because he didn't mean it as one, I was too simple to regard it as such, or too proud to reject it, still to this day, I can't say. However, I am thankful to him and everyone else who may have thought for a millisecond that calling me "Blacky" would decrease me—you amplified the very thing that has brought me to this moment.

Thank you to the indomitable women who crossed oceans, worked in factories as undocumented humans, fought back abusive husbands, built lives from dirt and water, and loved me into my full womanhood. You are my daily inspiration.

Thank you to my parents who love me like I am an only child and, so, allow me to live always on my own terms: Orelia C. Lewis and Luis M. DeSuze, I speak your name with an intense gratitude each day for how lucky I am to love and be loved by you.

To my uncles who told me my skin, smile, nails, teeth, lips, hair, eyes, and brain were beautiful before any other man could, Tios David DeSuze, Roberto Taylor, Samuel Lewis, and David Green. You gave me worth before the world could strip me of it.

To the People's Institute for Survival and Beyond—you wrote the manuscript and patiently taught me its lessons. To my Undoing Racism Internship Project crew—I fight so hard to keep us together because I love each of you that much and believe so deeply in the work.

Tangier Webb-Wallace, Cenita Adams Williamson, Kazim Weir, Joshua DeSuze, and Elizabeth Rossi—you affirm me in ways that give me life.

To Ryan Cameron, "well-behaved women seldom make history." (Laurel Thatcher Ulrich).

To those women who took me under their wings and picked up where my parents left off: Dr. Barbara Joseph, Candida Brooks-Harrison, Marianne Yoshioka, Susan Lob, Sally MacNichol, Athena Moore, Mimi Abramovitz, Terry Mizrahi, Sandra Bernabei, and Farah Tanis—it takes a village to raise an activist.

To the 'K' Tribe (you know who you are), despite all we have been through, I know I am because of you. And, to my DeSuze/Woolcock Tribe, I fight this fight for you.

To this Dream Team, Steve, Linda, and Mohan—this wasn't by accident. We were chosen for one another at this precise time to do this exact work—what a blessing.

As an eternal student waiting in expectation for my teachers, I give thanks to the people whose names I mentioned here and to all those who inspire me daily; while there is not enough space to list each name, love always.

(L. L.-B.): All thanks to God who has guided me through every step of my life. I am grateful to so many people who have encouraged and supported me, beginning with my family. Many thanks to my grandparents Candita and Gilberto Rosado who came to New York as young adults with barely a dollar in their pockets but a fistful of dreams which they imparted to their seven children, including my mother Josephine who believed that I could achieve things she couldn't imagine. Thanks to my father Damian who only achieved an eighth-grade education because he had to work but never stopped reading and learning because education happens every day, everywhere. Thanks to my younger brother Dae who looked up to me and, in doing so, inspired me to keep moving forward.

Many thanks to my husband Marshall and my children, all of whom are committed to the practice of starting and participating in difficult but necessary conversations. Marshall, we were brought together by God. We are two sides of the same coin, and in our journey together we are discovering our purpose and value. We are blessed with this blended group of special children: Antoine, the eldest, the architect who builds houses and communities on a foundation of equity, leading the team of siblings with his powerhouse wife Zawadi, an entrepreneur par excellence; Dyami, the artist who makes it a point to expand his lens through travel and art forms that communicate powerfully; Gabriel, the activist who literally fights every day against injustice in the streets of Philadelphia; Gideon, the engineer who with his brilliant wife Kim, a proud social worker, models the beauty and dignity of the young black family; Sara, the educator who sows seeds of love and justice in everything she does; Little Alice, the rising star; and Jasmine Yesenia who has barely been on the planet two decades but has committed herself to conversations on racism and identity with such humanity. In your eyes I am all I could ever want to be.

Thanks to Steve Burghardt, a mentor since my days at the Hunter School of Social Work, for this privilege of working with you and learning with you and Pat Beresford, a dear, true friend of my soul. Thank you to my dear colleagues at the NYU Silver School of Social Work and to my students from whom I learn every day. I extend my love and gratitude for my sister friends of a lifetime, Lynne, Marcy, Laura, Bernie, Candi, Darcel, Deidre, Arlene, Suzie Q., and Bonita. You've blessed me with your love and support.

Lastly, I dedicate this to all of the beautiful people, like Philando Castile, whose lives have been taken because their humanity was denied. May this book help to multiply the team of everyday crusaders who engage in conversations that allow us to recognize the shared humanity in each of us.

(M. V.): I am grateful to the many people who have taught, guided, and supported me throughout my life. I thank my partner Steve, who has helped me express my voice and has shown me that two people can make a relationship anything they want it to be. I thank my parents Usha and Gopala, who have given me a strong spiritual foundation from which I grow every day. I am blessed with a large, vibrant extended family and beautiful friends whom I treasure. I often tell my students that the many teachers who have inspired me are standing there with me as I sit in front of them. In particular, I want to thank my friend and mentor Steve Burghardt, who, from the first day I stepped into his class, encouraged me to share my ideas and has given me so many wonderful opportunities to grow as a social worker and writer—the latest being this book. I thank my dissertation advisor, Mimi Abramovitz, who believed in me and my purpose, especially at those times when I forgot what I was about and wanted to give up on myself. I thank Patricia Click, my former professor and advisor at the University of Virginia, who almost 30 years ago gave me the permission to pursue the spark inside me that said I needed to be a teacher. And I thank Susan Rogers, who gave me my first opportunity to teach. Finally, thank you to my students and colleagues at Lehman College. It is a joy and privilege to teach and learn with you.

FOREWORD

We are in a critical time in history, an era of challenge and turbulence for people throughout the world. During the past few years we have experienced or witnessed horrific instances of racial and ethnic violence in the US and abroad, challenging environmental conditions, and political instability. Continuing changes in local and global economies have contributed to growing economic and social inequality, and neoliberal public policies have charged the private sector, which puts profits over people, to address these conditions. Social workers and other social justice advocates need effective tools to build human and social capital, while continuing, as Martin Luther King Jr. famously said, to "bend the arc of history toward justice." A key element for this work is the ability to expand critical consciousness and awareness so we can bridge differences and work toward our collective good. A society, and world, that is polarized by difference can't address the magnitude of this project.

This book, which is grounded in dialogue between activist scholars and educators with different positionalities, contributes to this "tool box" of strategies and methods we can use to engage in constructive dialogue to educate others and ourselves due to this work. Social work educators have a critical role in educating students to do justice work in our communities and world, as "challenging social injustice" and "preventing and eliminating domination, exploitation, and discrimination" based on different social identities are key aspects of our professional mission. We need to develop these tools ourselves and model them in our interactions with students—both inside and outside of our classrooms. This means preparing our students to work toward justice, while managing the different social positionalitites that exist in our schools and classrooms. This guide contributes to this important project.

In 2007 the conservative National Association of Scholars (NAS) attacked our field for "indoctrinating" our students to adopt "progressive" perspectives. Although this attack was not successful in changing the focus of our programs, it did provide an opportunity for us, as a field, for self-examination and larger discussion regarding what we mean by diversity, social justice, and inclusivity. This attack on our field and our schools also revealed who among us might fight back, who might fear attack, and who might not truly share a common vision for our purpose as professional educators.

A Guide for Sustaining Conversations on Racism, Identity, and Our Mutual Humanity is very honest and transparent regarding what we face and what we must to do sustain ourselves as social justice educators. It is particularly helpful in pointing out how our different social identities and positionalities will impact this. Those of us whose identities are not at the center of our institutions or communities, who differ in social power and status from those we teach, will have different experiences from those with different identities. My hope is that this work will promote empathy across difference and can contribute to greater support for those of us who are often at the front lines of this work.

Of course, this magnitude of change requires work on every level. This guide emphasizes the important work that must occur within and between individuals, within groups, and within classrooms. It challenges how we may think about teaching, the place of "process" and "content," and how we handle emotion and affect in education. How interpersonal perceptions impact the way communications are understood and received. These are significant contributions.

But an equally important contribution occurs in these discussions, however brief, of the organizational contexts in which teaching and dialogue occur. It points out the significance of strong leadership, resources, and support on every level. It speaks to the importance of addressing our reward structures and tools of assessing teaching performance. Dialogue and intra-individual work are important, but without structural support, and change, within our institutions the impact of this work will be limited.

Each era presents its own challenges, and this era is particularly challenging. If we, as educators, intend to equip our students to work toward justice, we need to be able to create brave, not safe, spaces in our classrooms where different views and students with different identities are supported and can learn from each other. We need to focus more on "calling people in" for discussion, rather than "calling them out" when they voice dissenting or different views. We need to be able to understand what SW scholars Schulman and Gitterman describe as the "hidden group in the classroom" that can undermine or support our efforts toward genuine communication and learning. And we need to address the ways in which faculty members with marginalized identities are viewed by students and colleagues and how this can affect their success.

I am pleased that *A Guide for Sustaining Conversations on Racism, Identity, and Our Mutual Humanity* provides some insights and tools that can assist us in doing this kind of work, so that we, and current and future colleagues, can continue the work toward justice and positive change.

Lorraine Gutierrez
Arthur F. Thurnau Professor
Chair, Personality and Social Contexts
Department of Psychology
Core Faculty, Latino Studies Program
College of Literature, Science and Arts
Professor and Director of Diversity, Equity and Inclusion
School of Social Work
University of Michigan

INTRODUCTION

I. Origin of the Guide

In the current political, economic, and social atmosphere, fear, anger, and uncertainty seem to be everywhere. Divisions arise even in the midst of good intentions. Good people, particularly professors and agency supervisors, are not sure what to do when facing discussions on race, racism, and identity. Most faculty want a way forward but are not sure how to get there. The reality is that there are different responses for different people—for example, how a white person responds as opposed to a woman of color—and yet "flight or fight" is not the answer for anybody. These varied responses are a function of the many details that make us different in the first place—our culture, our values, our learned approaches to conflict, and our fears about real or perceived threats to name a few. Some people choose to withdraw from discussions on charged subjects while others may roll up their sleeves, ball up their fists, and prepare to fight. Some may respond inauthentically, hiding their true feelings while others move right into the arena of discomfort and put themselves at risk by sharing what they really think. We probably all lean towards one of these approaches even if we make exceptions at times. What is at stake here is not just any individual's level of comfort or discomfort, but how we make progress on the challenging issues of our time.

A Guide to Sustaining Conversations on Racism, Identity and Our Mutual Humanity is a hands-on "how-to" guide for teachers, students, agency professionals, and others wherever we work and live who seek to address the often daunting challenges of skillfully responding to difficult situations found today, manifested in settings such as classrooms and workplaces. These conversations matter—a lot—anywhere that people come together seeking answers and accountability on all-too-often overlooked topics such as:

- Race, power, and privilege in the classroom, workplace, boardroom: How do these potentially explosive issues impact the classroom or workplace? How do you respond when some speak negatively about others' perceived privilege?

- Handling the "Oppression Olympics": How do you handle different forms of social oppression besides race? Does one social identity "win" over another?
- Microaggressions vs. honest disagreement: How do you help students and others in workplaces and coalitions distinguish between the two?
- Measuring performance fairly and equitably: How do you handle differences in academic preparation where structural issues of race and class may have caused some students to arrive in your classroom less skilled than some of their classmates?
- How do you respond to the very different emotions that certain topics might raise—guilt in some socially and economically advantaged students, anger in some who have experienced systematic oppression throughout their lives?
- How do you maintain focus on the classroom content while responding to the above social issues in ways that create an academically rigorous, safe space for students to see the classroom as an engaging learning environment?

This guide offers one of many possible paths forward to dive deeply into these questions.

II. Our Paths to the Work

The four authors range from teachers of research, community organization, clinical practice, and field education—in short, the content areas that capture the breadth of a professional social work education and, indirectly, much of American work life in social services and education. Each team member also has been involved in some agency life as an executive, clinician, front line worker, organizer, or consultant. Like most groups of people, despite commonality, we each arrive at this work from different paths carrying a multitude of intersecting identities, which have informed our individual experiences as they relate to this material. At the core, you will find contrasting stories woven together by a deep commitment to work with and through these issues as part of our life's work. As we have celebrated and affirmed our diversity, we hope readers will also celebrate the differences and similarities that tie us to this journey: The human whole is greater than the sum of our parts.

III. The Process

Directly and compassionately addressing racism is often gritty and most certainly, varied. Because of our differences, we all agreed that it was important to honor how deeply personal, political, and consequential these issues are when they appear in the classroom, in faculty meetings, and in the field. In that spirit, we decided to systematically talk them through rather than pursue an intellectual endeavor. The actual language and approach used by us involved emotion as well as intellect. At the end of the day, we learned, and hope you will, too, to agree that no one approach fits all—indeed, it cannot. In this guide, you will find four approaches to the same questions, bound together by our respect for those approaches and the underlying connection to our mutual humanity.

This guide will provide answers to these and the other difficult questions that consistently confront faculty and supervisors in today's tumultuous and diverse world so that they engage in and sustain these conversations in their own classrooms and offices. The guide is a hands-on effort undertaken by four experienced, anti-racist educators and practitioners. These authors have, through trial and error, deep personal reflection, and sustained practice each developed a number of approaches to answer these questions in ways that greatly diminish both dogma and fear in classrooms and replace them with ongoing, mutually supportive learning environments. While united in this commitment, as individuals, the four authors are necessarily diverse. After all, how one responds to the above questions—and how students respond to each faculty member as well—is necessarily different for a young, untenured Afro-Latina and an older, White, full professor. By examining how socially different people respond to the same difficult question, the guide seeks to create a rich set of options for the readership to utilize in their own classrooms, agencies, and field placements.

We accomplished this not by a traditional intellectual endeavor through literature reviews and new research but by carrying on sustained, experientially based conversations among the four authors. Each chapter is built around a difficult question with the four engaging in the give-and-take of commonalities and differences that appear in response. As such, the work models ways to express differences that enrich rather than impede dialogue and to do so through "lessons learned" and "approaches taken" that will resonate with socially diverse faculty.

The work may also surprise you, for what emerges here also addresses something else—our own humanity and how it is challenged and stretched inside and outside the classroom or office. For weeks, we committed to bearing witness to our individual and collective discovery process. As a group, we experienced laughter, joy, and pain and suffering, too. Most of all, we experienced new aspects of our own humanity as well as that of one another. It was truly humbling.

IV. Format to the Guide

The conversations were broken into three areas:

Part One: "Before We Enter the Classroom" features a dialogue about the personal, community, and institutional infrastructure necessary in a program to make these conversations authentic, sustainable, and meaningful.

Part Two: "The Classroom Conversations" features the hot-button questions that many faculty have asked for support to further bolster their ability to appropriately respond in the classroom.

Part Three: "Shifting the Teaching Paradigm" features lessons for critical pedagogy, classroom management, and learning.

V. A Final Invitation to the Reader

We invite readers to journey with us. We ask that you enter our humanity. We ask that you remember this guide is an authentic dialogue between colleagues and friends who are experts in their own subjective experiences. Our own lesson is there is no such thing as a "right" question in the classroom as it relates to race, racism, sexuality, heterosexism, gender, sexism, socioeconomic status, and classism. These are deeply personal topics that reach back into collective yet starkly unique individual histories as we explore our own stories, vulnerability, and resilience. We invite you to do the same. As you do so, let's support one another in cultivating:

- Patience to deal with your development
- Willingness to take risks
- Commitment to authenticity
- Letting go of perfectionism
- Acknowledging internalized racial superiority and inferiority and, in doing so, forgiving ourselves and one another
- Leaning in with curiosity
- Remembering that it's all in the little things, not one big thing, that keeps the work alive and the capacity to keep growing for us all. This guide is an invitation to do just that.

PART ONE:
BEFORE WE ENTER THE CLASSROOM

CONVERSATION ONE

Question: How can I create safety in the classroom, respecting the balance between harmony and disharmony needed for learning?

Background to this conversation:
This conversation centers around the following reflective questions that colleagues have raised over the years as we all struggle to make our classrooms powerful, accountable, and open learning environments.

Observations and Reflections:
- *The concept of "safe space" often connotes the avoidance of risk and conflict, which then impedes the cultivation of authentic relationships. We need to challenge the concept of "safe spaces." If we can shift the paradigm from "safe space" to "accountable space," what would that look like in terms of building relationships in a classroom?*
- *In our roles as instructors, we wield power and authority in the classroom. How do we relate to this authority? What are we willing and unwilling to let go of in terms of that authority?*
- *As human beings, we have a tendency to try to keep ourselves safe. What do I do as an instructor to try to keep myself "safe" (in the sense of self-protection)? What do I do to challenge my sense of safety in order to grow?*

THE CONVERSATION

Mohan: Our first question is: *How can I create safety in the classroom, respecting the balance between harmony and disharmony needed for learning?* Safety is something that I'm always thinking about as a teacher. Maybe because, in ways, I felt safe being in the classroom, and then there are also many ways that I felt unsafe. I guess I'm always very sensitive to safety. I think this question relates very specifically to when I taught a new course a few years ago on social work with lesbian, gay, bisexual, transgender, queer and, questioning (LGBTQ) populations. It was the first time a class like this was offered to social work students at the college where I teach.

This question really came alive in that class. It made me think about what creates a safe environment for people to really wrestle with things and to really face things in themselves. When I did a research study after the class to find out about the students' experience, safety came out as a theme. As I started thinking about this question more, I started to ask myself: Safety from what? Is it criticism? Is it disrespect? What is it? It made me think. I keep using this word "safety" all the time, but then I asked myself again today, Safety from what? I don't know what it is. I want to pose that question.

I want to go back to what bell hooks says about this idea of a transformative learning space. My understanding of bell hooks is that she challenges the idea that in order for a place to be safe, it needs to be harmonious. She says in *Teaching to Transgress*: "Recognition of difference might also require of us a willingness to see the classroom change to allow for shifts in relations between students." She goes on to say it's difficult for individuals to shift paradigms and that there must be a setting for folks to voice fears, to talk about what they are doing, how they are doing it, and why. To me, maybe safety is, how do you create an environment where people can be okay with being scared? That's what it resonates. She says that we can't do this alone. We have to create a community.

That is, it is the community that creates the safety. Reading her work challenged me to think that I place too much responsibility on myself. I need to let the community form, and then that community can maybe help us to feel safe to be scared.

Linda: I love the question. *Safe from what?* I think that would be a great conversation to have in the classroom to really examine what are some of the unspoken expectations that students have about being safe and who's going to keep them safe. Whose job is it to keep them safe? I think what people may be seeking is to be safe from discomfort. I think one of the ways to approach this is to embed the notion of discomfort right into the pedagogy, to establish it as an expectation right from the beginning—that learning comes with discomfort because it requires stretching. It requires growing. It requires grappling with unfamiliar ideas. By definition, discomfort is part of the learning process. You're normalizing the discomfort. You're setting it up as an expectation that it's a condition of the classroom experience.

You set ground rules, norms, parameters around the way discomfort can be expressed and the way we can support each other through that discomfort but it's weaved right into the learning process. We establish that as an expectation.

Steve: I love what you said about discomfort because to me, that's really the heart of learning. At the beginning of the school year, in my experience, what I find is that students initially, because they're so uncomfortable just being in graduate school or undergraduate school, they're always on best behavior. Like you said, Linda, it's the best time to remind students that later in the term they're not going to be so well-behaved. Early on, we therefore need to establish how we want to be together

> *Embed the notion of discomfort right into the pedagogy ... establish it as an expectation right from the beginning—that learning comes with discomfort because it requires stretching. It requires growing. It requires grappling with unfamiliar ideas. By definition, discomfort is part of the learning process. You're normalizing the discomfort. You're setting it up as an expectation that it's a condition of the classroom experience.*

when those hard times come. If we're into learning, the learner at some point is going to have "ouch" moments that are going to cause people that discomfort. People will be triggered, and that means some people potentially are going to respond very negatively to each other.

Especially in my practice classes, I have not had an experience where at some point in the year, somebody didn't get really upset with at least one other student. That's the moment where these ground rules become really, really important. Back at the start of the term, students never want to follow them at first. My experience is people just want to get on with "learning." They want to know what they need to know to *do* good work. As a professor, it took me awhile to get comfortable enough to say, "No, we need to pause. We need to first establish how do we want to approach each other? How do we really want to handle our responses if somebody says something that hurts us based on our own identity or our own story?"

By the way, besides creating that atmosphere of discomfort that both of you have spoken to, I want to begin to establish a little authority within the students. Discipline is up to us all.

As you were saying, Mohan, that is not all on me. The authority comes from all of us. When these things later happen, and they do, a student gets to step in because of these rules and not wait for the prof. I have a good example of this. A student last week in class, a white woman, spoke with the jargon of a young person of color at her placement in a way that a number of students felt was demeaning. Because we have the ground rules, a young woman of color was able to say, "Ouch," and "The way that landed, it hurt me." She didn't call her a racist or say that what she said sounded like a racist. She may have *felt* that way, but instead of responding that way, she used the ground rules to get this older white woman to pause and really think a lot about this. Instead of all hell breaking loose, it created a really healthy, difficult, uncomfortable, and real conversation.

Kalima: I want to challenge this idea of safety. I wonder if we can even create that and how real it is. I ground my spaces in the same way you just talked about, Linda. However, I add that we need to get comfortable with the idea of being uncomfortable. That's just part of this work. It's going to be part of this work in the classroom. It's going to be part of the work in your practice. There's going to be many times in our practice, whether we're at the direct-service level, community level, or policy level where we are going to be uncomfortable for a very long period of time. We just have to get comfortable with that idea of discomfort and lack of control.

> *We need to get comfortable with the idea of being uncomfortable.*

The fact is, there will never be a time when the space is completely safe for everyone. I move more towards an accountable space, which is using the ground rules to hold us all accountable to an ethic of who we want to be in the world and how we want to show up.

When I say accountable, just using your example, that was an accountable moment. She was accountable to her own feelings and experience by saying, "Ouch," and not placing the blame on anyone, just inviting conversation.

The other thing that I wanted to bring up is this idea of transferring authority. My teaching philosophy is based on the ideas of three books: *Teaching to Transgress*, bell hooks; *Pedagogy of the Oppressed*, Paulo Freire; and *The People's History*, Howard Zinn ("The Coming Revolt of the Guards").

One of the things that Zinn has said is that "you can't be neutral on a moving train." I already know the classroom is inherently a political space. As such, it is a space of contention if I am pushing towards liberation. It is a space of discomfort manifested by our own awakening if I'm pushing towards self-awareness and deepening. This requires a specific type of relationship, one where there is trust in the process of being with one another.

Modeling this idea of being in an authentic relationship in the classroom is a very, very difficult task in terms of what you referred to in transferring authority. It's so difficult and scary.

Part of that is, we're going to make mistakes. It's going to hurt. We're not going to like each other some days. Other days, we're going to love each other. That's just inherently the core of what it means to be in an authentic relationship. That can also exist in a classroom. Just like in our relationships, it's not safe per se because we are two human beings making mistakes all the time. However, we must be accountable.

We have to be able to be accountable with our own feelings. If somebody says something that hurts, we say, "Ouch, that hurts." That person gets to be accountable to us and to our community and say, "Oh, I am sorry. This is what I meant ... " moving the relationship forward.

If I tell somebody that it's going to be safe, and then it's not, then what happens? The final thing I wanted to say is I like this question of "Safety from what?" and whose responsibility it is to create safety? I think you brought that up, Mohan. What I do in the beginning is ask three questions, and I make students put their answers in different shapes and different colors on the board. In a circle, I say, "What do you need from this class so you can show up as your 100% self or as close to 100%?" In a box, "What are your expectations, your highest expectations of this experience?" In a heart, "Who do you intend to be to manifest the two things that you want?" I absolve myself from this idea of safety or creating something that they want and instead intentionally invite them to the process of co-creating the space and experience they are declaring.

If someone writes "humble," it's what you need to be. I did not promise that nor did I prescribe that behavior to you. It's your declaration; you own it. My hope and expectation is that they will then show up as humbly as possible in the learning process so that they can manifest exactly what they want from the experience and be who they have said they want to be. I just don't think that we can manifest or create safety the way they want it. They have to be responsible for it, too.

Mohan: From the three of you, I circled three key ideas which are really helping me think about all of this. I'm frankly getting bored of this whole idea of safety. I'm boring myself for thinking about safety. I'm liking all these other ways of thinking about it. I guess to take one point from each of you, I love the idea, Linda, about unspoken expectations, this idea of setting expectations together with the students about how we can express ourselves, how we can support each other. I like that way of thinking about expectations. The whole thing about transferring authority, which we've also been speaking about, is something I think I've struggled with ever since I started teaching. I'm just thinking about the classroom. I'm teaching again this LGBTQ elective this semester to the undergraduates.

In my undergraduate LGBTQ elective this semester, I did something similar to what you, Kalima, talked about in terms of having the students reflect on what they can offer and what they need to create this idea of a safe space. One of my colleagues likes the concept "risk friendly" rather than safe space. I talk to my students about what that means, risk friendly. What does it mean to have a risk-friendly environment? This whole idea of transferring authority, there's still something that doesn't sit right with me with the way I conduct a class. There is a role to play as the facilitator. There's a reason I'm there. I can't just be like, "Here's the topic," and I walk out of the room. There's a reason. It's like group therapy. Sometimes the group therapist sits there and says nothing the entire time. If you remove that person, the therapeutic process won't happen.

The process requires that focal point who is the instructor. There's something about me being the conduit through which things go which isn't sitting right with me. I've always struggled with this. Balancing the responsibility, I have to be that whatever you call it, maybe a conduit, a facilitator. There are times I'm going to be lecturing. I have that role, too. How do I balance that and do it in a way that doesn't short circuit the process that happens between my students? I guess maybe I'm thinking about this transfer of authority even more now. To your point, Kalima, about accountability, I love that idea of moving from a safe space to an accountable space. Reframing that notion, I find that really helpful.

Linda: It's a process. If you go see a therapist, that's a process. If you're in a classroom, that's a process. I think that there has to be "contracting" that has to take place about what's going to happen in *this* process, in *this* space. People bring expectations into those other processes I mentioned. They may be thinking, "This is what it's going to be like. I'm going to come. You know things that I don't know. You're going to teach them to me.

You're going to deposit them into me and I'm going to leave more enlightened." I think we need to try to bring those expectations out into the open, to the surface, and then engage in a re-contracting process that turns that on its ear. You establish that you're not the sole authority here or the only leader here. Everybody here has a responsibility of bringing leadership to this process.

There is something about the way the classroom is set up that reinforces the idea of one instructor with all of the knowledge. It mimics and mirrors all of the things we are fighting to change in society. The authority figure with the power is at the front of the room, and everyone else is passively waiting for the edict to come on down so they can know. We have to challenge that, but students need to be aware, to be made conscious of that, so we should make them aware of that and re-contract about what it's going to be like. Otherwise, it's very parental in a way.

Even the notion of creating safety is very parental. It assumes we can actually do that, as though safety is ours to give. It reminds me of what we talk about in social work—empowerment. We act like it's ours to give. Is it? It doesn't belong to us. The revolution has to start before any of the lessons start. It has to start with breaking, shattering ideas of what this learning space is supposed to be and coming to a revised understanding of what that is. You're starting with disruption to begin with. How can we start with disruption and make it safe at the same time? If we promise that, we're kidding ourselves, and we're kidding them."

Kalima: You can't do both at the same time.

Steve: That's great about the disruption. I'm thinking a lot about how students initially perceive what they're going to get out of their educational experience. What's been unacknowledged? What's been unacknowledged is that they expect that there's going to be a lot of authority at the front of the room. That they're going to be deposits from the professor on whatever her or his great learning is. My take on this, frankly, as the older white guy who is having them read my own text, to expect anything different towards me at first would be unfair to them.

What the ground rules are meant to do, as you're saying, is to disrupt a little. It's just a little. Begin to get them to gnaw at the idea that the only authority is me. I have to have patience about how long it takes to alter that relationship because it's not going to happen right away. It's going to be a little bit here and a little bit later, especially as mistakes are made.

One thing that's always important is when I make a mistake. I wouldn't say a grievous error but inevitably I overstate something or my data is a little more out of date. There'll be some student with great nervousness who says, "Dr. B., I'm not sure but maybe ... " and it's that moment of truth about whether or not I respect their authority or I use it to say, "Well, thank you for sharing, but my point of view really is more important here. I'm going to keep going." When their challenge is respected, then things shift; it begins altering the authority of where learning can happen even more.

The ground rules, if used correctly, I can respond in kind. Somebody says, "Ouch," and I go, "I didn't mean to do that." It doesn't completely do away with my authority nor do I expect it to, but it alters our relationship a bit. That's important because like a client-worker relationship, the entire relationship's going to be altered in a relatively short period of time. It can be shifted so that people later reinterpret what they can do in the world. That time of re-interpretation is a big deal, and a teacher has to plan for that early on by believing that students have the capacity to do so.

The other concrete thing, just about the ground rules part, I don't take a huge amount of time in the first class. I take a little time over two or three classes so that it gets people to be thinking about it before they make it a contract. I make them come clear on if you're saying "respect," what's the behavior associated with respect? If you're saying "support," what's the behavior associated with support?

That forces people to become reflective. Out of that we begin to get to—Kalima, what you said—the idea of a mutual accountability to each other and not just to me. Then, when the class breaks down at Week 6, people are able to deal with it pretty well.

Kalima: Something about what you said triggered a thought I've been considering for quite some time. Every time we talk about safety, I feel like we're always talking about the students. We never talk about us. What does it mean for us to feel completely human? We teach *Pedagogy of the Oppressed*, and we somehow leave ourselves out of it. I am an absolute mess every single day, I'm just a mess. People think that I'm organized. I'm really not all that organized. I will be in the building one door down from the classroom and still get there late. That's just my life. How do we set it up where we get to be as human as they do? The truth is, humanity is sometimes not extended to us. The class is not set up in this way. Instead, I feel like I live in a reality where I am expected to have all the answers, or I have to know everything. I absolutely cannot. White, male, heterosexist ideals of perfection create an environment in which we're almost forced to assume a completely dehumanizing posture. I often imagine and try hard to practice, true accountability and active, intentional power sharing. The allowance for humanity can look like that if it were afforded to us as well.

How do we begin to build that in? I build it in with a podcast. It's called Making Mistakes: TED Radio Hour. (You may access this podcast by pasting the following link into your browser: http://www.npr.org/2013/03/11/174030515/making-mistakes). My aim is to normalize mistakes, and if I'm lucky, the class will even begin to honor its role and value missteps in our collective journey.

This sets the stage for me to show my full human self. Whatever that may be—it could be as simple as not having a pen. Can that simple thing be received as a reflection of my humanity rather than a marker of my competence?

For folks of color and/or those of us who fall outside dominant and favored identities, this is truly a risk. I never know how I will be perceived. The truth is, I can't waste my time, energy, or mental health trying to control it. If I am to undo what has been done to our way of relating, if I am to truly reach to create a liberatory space, then I have to try to create a classroom that prioritizes our complete humanity before we even get started on a "lesson"—before we crack open any textbook. Let's just talk about humanity and go from there.

Guiding Principles and Strategies

Students and faculty come into the classroom with expectations, both spoken and unspoken, both conscious and unconscious. By naming and talking about these expectations, we can begin to co-create an environment of mutual accountability. In order to create an accountable space, all of the teachers and all of the learners in the room need to make the implicit curriculum explicit. There is an expanded power in naming that which has gone unnamed for too long.

- Principle: Discomfort is a necessary condition for transformative learning.
- Strategy: Establish an explicit expectation through initial contracting that discomfort will be experienced and identify guidelines/processes (like "ouch") for how it will be expressed and how we can support one another.

It takes time to create an accountable space. Classes, like all relationships, have beginnings, middles, and endings. While co-creating safety and accountability requires intentional efforts, there is also the need to let it emerge over time. We cannot force it or demand it.

- Principle: Safety is not ours to give. Teachers can only create the conditions in which a classroom community can become accountable to one another for learning.
- Strategy: Accept the limits of your power as a teacher and trust the power of the class to co-create an accountable space for learning that will emerge and strengthen over the life of the class. The moment we enter into a space together, there is a disruption, and this disruption is often unsettling. Academics all too often have come up with ways to try to smooth, soften, and manage that which is inherently disrupting, particularly within classroom settings. Acknowledge and gradually learn to embrace the disruption.
- Principle: Your honesty and humility about what you don't know is itself a teaching tool.
- Strategy: Accept the limits of your knowledge base and allow students to teach you and each other from their lived experiences. Dare to exercise leadership by creating a learning space where knowledge is co-created. Model curiosity, humility, and openness. Be a student and a teacher.

CONVERSATION TWO

Question: *How much do I self-disclose in the classroom setting? When is it appropriate? How does that impact my authenticity if I am asking students to be open and vulnerable?*

Background to this conversation:
This conversation emerged among faculty who struggle with the historic professional expectation of clear boundaries with little to no exposing of personal information. Such boundary setting runs up against the anti-oppression expectation that "we model the change we seek," which Gandhi espoused in building powerful social movements among the disempowered.

Observations and Reflections:
There are obvious differences in the professor's role between practice-based courses and orienting-knowledge courses such as Human Behavior and the Social Environment and Social Welfare Policy. At the same time, helping reveal social dynamics that come into play in each classroom is the responsibility of every faculty member. How powerful a difference on boundary setting is there among faculty? Is it a significant one, or only a matter of degree? In addition, some of the reflective questions that emerged are:

- *If we are asking students to interrogate their own stories and how those stories reveal social dynamics tied to power and privilege, can they not ask the same from us?*
- *If we are creating ground rules where authority is being dispersed and deconstructed, don't we have to both expect and respect possible push back from students about our own social makeup and how we have handled uncomfortable social issues in our own lives?*
- *How far do we go with respecting an "accountable space" that includes faculty in the class's personal narrative without relinquishing boundaries still needed for grading and evaluation?*

THE CONVERSATION

Steve: Kalima, I think that's so important to raise the issue of our common humanity as we move to this next question, which is *How much do I self-disclose? When is it appropriate? How does that impact my authenticity if I'm asking students to be open and vulnerable?* I know for myself, in terms of self-disclosure, the point you just made about humanity is really critical. I don't start there too early because one of the things I don't want to foster is what I call "abstract intimacy," which is where people share too much of themselves before I barely know their name.

Mohan: I've had that kind of thing happen, too.

Steve: We don't want to go that far. I know you're not speaking about that, Kalima, but what I do is I begin with the obvious self-disclosure about me. It always creates reaction. I'll say, "Well, here it is, another class, and now I'm the older white guy in the front of the room." I've never had the response where some people don't giggle nervously because of me stating the obvious about me being white. For 40 years, people have always giggled! That's because part of what I'm doing through this obvious disclosure is laying the foundation for our needed discomfort and the kind of conversations that are going to happen.

Which conversations? The conversations that everybody really wants to have and nobody does with any consistency, which are the dynamics about how race shows up or other parts of our social identity that show up every day, wherever we are. Those conversations in turn create conflict and discomfort, especially if we're not really open to the vulnerability, as you said, about our humanity. By naming some of my social identity *and not making it a big deal*, I am expecting people to laugh. I've only worked at this for 40 years! I'm not uncomfortable any more. At the same time, there are people who are. I'm not asking them to really jump in with that. What I try to do is tell them to stay with wherever you're comfortable with your discomfort. Not just with your discomfort but where you're authentic. You're authentic in the vulnerability you feel. That's the level of disclosure you should do.

This term, I have a student who said, "I'm an orphan student. I grew up all white and Jewish in my community. I went to a school that was primarily for Jewish students. I've never been in East Harlem, and I admit at times, I'm scared." She is much more vulnerable and honest about what she's attempting to deal with than some of the students who abstractly and "correctly" parrot whatever the particular issue of the day is. She's real about where she actually is as opposed to where she thinks she ought to be. For me, necessary self-disclosure begins with something that has a social dimension. It's meant to tie into people's awareness of accepting a level of vulnerability they can tolerate and not back away from. If you demand too much, they can't do it.

If you don't demand anything at all, you're failing to do what you said, which is for people to eventually get to the discourse about our messy issues that overlay our common humanity.

Kalima: When I think about self-disclosure, I think about the tactical use of self in my classrooms. How am I using myself as a way to challenge power, re-imagine what power could look like in the classroom, challenge their ideas of who I am. How am I using myself to challenge the ideas of blackness, challenge the ideas of whatever single story they created of me because I carry a particular aesthetic. The natural hair, contemporary dresses in African prints, big bangles, headwraps, ankle bracelets, no make up, scented with oils—all of this sets up a space where an entire story is created without my consent. Oftentimes, it is a romanticized version of me and my reality. I wonder if I fill some role of the "good" black—earthy, grounded, and deserving of respect—it would serve me well to sit comfortably in that space; my ego and probably my evaluations would love the feeling. However, I am aware of the danger inherent in this false reality. It almost places me out of reach, yet I remain anchored by blackness in my reality and theirs. When I say anchored, I don't allow myself to be confused; my blackness anchors me in a harsh reality that as much as they may like my style, I am still a black woman, and if I ever "step out of line," threatened whiteness will engage that anchor at any moment to bring me tumbling down.

I feel like for some students, this demand for perfection is pervasive and unconscious. I think this is the only way they know how to be in a relationship—by putting somebody up on a pedestal or expecting perfection. My tactical use of self means I slowly just take a step down each classroom until we are all just a mess together. I name the pedestal. I name the truth about the "good black," the process of romanticizing, the evoking of white privilege when things don't go their way. I name it all, and I am able to do this because I ground them in specific readings that speak to my ancestry and our shared history, particularly as it relates to the academy: bell hooks, *Teaching to Transgress*.

First of all, I start them off with this particular reading that says, this is who I am, and this is my style of facilitation.

I use the pieces of my story that I know they need to hear to move the conversation forward, to model vulnerability. My hope each class is that sharing these strategically chosen little bits and pieces of my identity, about my struggle, about my reality allows for a different type of relationship to power and to the work of liberation. It's not painted as this nice picture. In fact, it's an unfinished imperfect picture that allows them to think deeper, feel deeper, and to see me differently and feel as if they're in relationship with me because I do want to be in relationship with them. To be certain, I do not offer up the tragic pieces of my life for scrutiny, analysis, or otherwise; I'm not roadkill. However, I share my "incomplete" status as often as the moment feels right to drive home a sense of what Brené Brown calls "wholeheartedness." (See Side Box 1.)

I've only had this backlash one time in six years of teaching. It was this older guy who was not fully comfortable in himself, with himself, and in this type of relationship. He needed me to be at the front of the classroom. I sit in the group. I don't sit in the front of the classroom. He needed me to have definitive answers all the time. I just didn't.

One day, he decided he was going to try it out because he was struggling with my facilitation style. He went overboard, and it was okay. I was like,

Box 1: Brené Brown's "Ten Guideposts for Wholeheartedness"

In her book, *Daring Greatly: How the Courage to Be Vulnerable Transforms the Way We Live, Love, Parent, and Lead*, Brené Brown says the ten characteristics shared by people living a "wholehearted life" are as follows:

1. Cultivating Authenticity: Letting Go of What People Think
2. Cultivating Self-Compassion: Letting Go of Perfectionism
3. Cultivating a Resilient Spirit: Letting Go of Numbing and Powerlessness
4. Cultivating Gratitude and Joy: Letting Go of Scarcity and Fear of the Dark
5. Cultivating Intuition and Trusting Faith: Letting Go of the Need for Certainty
6. Cultivating Creativity: Letting Go of Comparison
7. Cultivating Play and Rest: Letting Go of Exhaustion as a Status Symbol and Productivity as Self-Worth
8. Cultivating Calm and Stillness: Letting Go of Anxiety as a Lifestyle
9. Cultivating Meaningful Work: Letting Go of Self-Doubt and "Supposed To"
10. Cultivating Laughter, Song, and Dance: Letting Go of Being Cool and "Always in Control" (pp. 9–10)

"Okay. You went overboard. It's all right. Let's talk about it." In an opening exercise, we were discussing politics of domination and the way it sadly shows up in love. We were collectively commiserating about how badly this complicates our experiences of giving, receiving, and being in love. I shared how much I love *love*, yet struggle to sustain it. In my opinion, it's the universal dilemma, so not a huge leap. The whole classroom was in the circle with me in agreement. He then brought that up in a joking manner, about two classes later.

It was so inappropriate and such a sting to us all who ventured into the circle to be in community. There really was no need for him to bring it up because that was such an intimate space but because he's not used to being in a space like that where somebody he's labeled as his professor models vulnerability and community, he didn't know the boundaries. That's also probably my bad as well. I also feel when we want to talk about identity, the realest place to go to is our intimate relationships in our families. That's the space that I wanted them to go. We ended up having a lovely, lovely conversation. Again, how does my disclosure move the work forward and deeper? Shift in power. It doesn't always have to be students disclosing. I'm going to disclose a little bit, too.

Mohan: For me, this idea of tactical use of self, I think of it that way. I really love what you said earlier about what it takes for us to feel completely human. I think year after year of teaching, I'm becoming more of a human being in the classroom. I think I'm becoming more of a human being in general, allowing it to be messy, although I have to say then I also have a lot of defensiveness. There's still a lot of defenses that come up and not wanting to look foolish, not wanting to look like I'm not prepared. The worst thing that anybody can tell me is that I wasn't prepared. That brings up lots of humiliation and shame.

My knee-jerk reaction is to want to attack. The thing is, I found very crafty ways in a classroom to mask the attack. Something came up when I was preparing for today. I thought about an experience I had just last week actually in my LGBTQ elective. At one point, I was using the phrase, "racial minority." We were talking about language. We're talking a lot about language and labels and how are labels helpful, not helpful, and all that. I used this as an example of this idea, "What is a racial minority, especially when the demographics of this country are changing?" Then this young man raised his hand, very soft-spoken young man. I have my students write weekly journals. He came up to me after the first class and very softly said, "Professor, I don't think I did it right. I've never been asked to actually share my own opinion." He's not used to that.

I said, "I want to hear what you're thinking." Anyway, he raised his hand when I said racial minority. I believe he's a Latino young man, about my skin color. He made this beautiful statement about how regardless of demographics, there's still power in society, and there are people who are dominating. Whether the demographics change, there are still people who are discriminating. There's violence against people of color, but he said it in this beautiful way, which basically talked about power and oppression.

It was one of those moments where he, in his own way, was challenging my statement about racial minority. It wasn't in a hostile way or anything. In the past, I would have probably gotten more defensive in that moment. He was offering me a gift, and he offered the class a gift because I could then refer back to that statement for the whole class.

For me and all my classes, the issue of self-disclosure (see Side Box 2) comes up when I reveal to students that I'm gay. The relevance of that, the lack of relevance of

Box 2: Self-Disclosure

What is self-disclosure?
Self-disclosure refers to the helping professional, in this case the teacher, sharing personal opinions, thoughts, feelings, and details about one's life with the client, in this case students.
The ways in which teachers and students self-disclose necessarily differ based on one's real and perceived social identities.
For those from real and/or perceived social privilege:

- Early: A modest statement of one's social/racial identity (neither dwelled on nor denied)
- Later: Areas of incompletion (what you're not good at, as well as competent at)

It's also important to be aware of the risks of self-disclosure. These include:

- For privileged: Some colleagues may perceive you either as manipulating students to be well-liked or that you are "hung up" on racial and other social topics.
- Self-disclosure on the part of systemically marginalized folks can play into pre-existing stereotypes further complicating the relationship.

that. ... They can tell that I'm brown. They could tell that I'm Indian or some kind of Asian descent. People wouldn't necessarily know that I'm gay unless of course I refer to my partner. In this class, I made a decision in the second class that I was just going to come out. I guess when I was thinking more about this question, I was thinking of self-disclosure as self-disclosing facts about me and my background and all that. Then I was asking myself, aren't we self-disclosing all the time? What we choose to say or not to say, how we respond, how we behave, what readings we choose, the ways we evaluate students. I started to think this morning, "Wow, I'm self-disclosing all the time." I could have responded to that young man in a very different way, and I might have in another year. The way I respond is self-disclosing about me.

In a way, it made me think more broadly about self-disclosure as beyond disclosing facts about me. I'm constantly disclosing myself through my humanity and through my behaviors. I just wanted to put that out there. That led me to think about these dichotomies between personal and professional, academic and non-academic, intellectual and emotional. We create these splits. If we are to move in the direction of being completely human, how am I going to separate out my personal and professional? What does that mean? Separate out something that's emotional versus intellectual? This morning when I was preparing for this question, thinking about the splits, something about the self-disclosure question got me to think about these splits between things that we create—in the classroom, agency, everywhere, it could be any environment. I want to just throw that out there.

I think I'm realizing now that I am self-disclosing all the time, maybe not in the way that it's always talked about.

Linda: Whether you know it or not, whether you're aware or not, we are self-disclosing all the time. There are things we may think are hidden or removed. You're thinking, like, "Oh, they won't know that I've had a rough morning." You think it's not showing, but it may be. It may very well be evident.

I'm thinking about that separating out that we do in some roles. We are associated with being professional, and yet, what we profess to be going for is a learning experience that is integrated. We don't want them to learn in these silos. How could we possibly talk about an issue like race and compartmentalize it so that it stays only in an intellectual sphere? That's not possible. It doesn't reside only in an intellectual sphere. I think if you're going to make any progress on the issue at all, you better move out of an only intellectual space. You have to move into a personal space. As I'm listening to you, I'm thinking even though I would have always said I'm an advocate for being authentic, for bringing your whole self, I'm going to ratchet that up to say it's *imperative*.

It's imperative if you're going to have any conversation on race. If you're going to aim to not just impart facts and information, but you're aiming to transform yourself and other people—if that's the work you're in, then there's no way you can show up in only one dimension of yourself. It's just not possible. This conversation has also made me conscious of something that I probably wasn't before, which is that when I walk into a classroom, I feel like I'm already disrupting just by walking in because I don't represent the natural order of things. I'm not supposed to be the professor. Someone who looks like me is not supposed to be the professor. When I walk into a class in my brown skin, with my "black" (albeit permed) hair and introduce myself as Dr. Lausell Bryant, then right off the bat, there's a disruption right there. I think if we were to ask students in most American universities to close their eyes and share what image comes to mind when they hear the word "professor," I doubt the image would be one that resembles me, a brown-skinned Puerto Rican woman with a Ph.D. That said, I feel like it's an advantage. I think it's a very powerful advantage. I feel like immediately, there's going to be some curiosity.

"What are you doing here? What's your deal? How equipped are you to be at the front of the classroom? Let me see. Let me test that. What are you doing here in this particular institution where I'm paying $60,000+ a year? Which affirmative action truck did you fall off of to get here? Are you going to be good? Are you going to be what I think someone who fell off the affirmative action truck is like? Let's see." There is a part of me that thinks that is a great tool. I'm like, "Well, we're engaged now. It's on!" I think that right off the bat it gives me lots of teachable moments. I'm just conscious of the fact that I actually like that, that I experience it as something powerful.

Steve: How did you arrive at that? I certainly know people who have the opposite experience who tell me as a woman of color, as a man of color, that they try to avoid that subject—who they are—because of the very reason that people are going to perceive them as "less than." They're just going to go do the work the way it needs to be done.

Linda: What I'm becoming very aware of right now is that I think what I do is that I like to show that I am fully prepared. "We're going to get this out of the way really quick. I know my stuff. I'm prepared."

Steve: Just like Mohan said.

Linda: Then I'm going to hit you with my humanity. I was not aware I did that until I'm listening to you. That is what I do. That is how I feel.

Steve: It's so interesting you said that because I truly attempt to do the opposite for the very reasons of who I am and what my social identity is, which is I want them to know quickly a little bit about my humanity and my own lived experience. The other thing about being perceived as an incredibly smart white guy—I need to put that guy to rest. What I give them in one of my early classes, whether it's a class in Political Economy or a practice course, is the importance of not being perfect or expecting perfectibility. I say one of the things that freed me as a human being is from Paulo Freire's quotation that "to be fully human is being incomplete." I go on a little: "You're going to see many examples of my incompletions." For example, I say very early on, if it happens, "I forgot my pen." Here I go again. I don't like to write on the board. I'm a terrible writer. I admit it openly. I don't make a big deal about it. I don't do false humility.

False humility also means I don't deny who I am either—I am a successful person with work I'm proud of. At the same time, it's important for me, the fullness of who I am includes that some of me is a little bit of a mess. Not so much as to be fake, but what you were saying, Mohan, about all those other things about the syllabus, about the choice of readings, the way I'm dressed, and all those things communicate something about me anyway. What you're saying is so important. I feel the need, and this is because different people have to show up in different ways around the same material. You and I cannot do exactly the same. If I show up as overly super-prepared, I only reinforce the structure of white supremacy that I have no interest in supporting. If you as a person of color show up with your humanity of incompletion first, the white supremacy that people have experienced unconsciously suddenly begins to write you off.

Each of us has to be aware that there's a different dynamic in play that we have to be willing to take on. There's no cookie cutter. The wonderful thing about the former is we're all different. Thank God for that.

Linda: We show up based on that lived experience. For me, I've got to first make sure you're clear that I'm qualified and prepared to be here. Once we understand that, I'm going to give you my full humanity because I have to hold those two things together all the time. I can't just be human and not be prepared. That's not going to fly.

Mohan: For me, sometimes I'll go in, and I'll have my notes that I've written and this plan. Then I think there's a part of me that's … I want my students to show up. I want to show up in the moment. The phrase that's coming to mind as you're all talking right now is about being in the moment, being present. I think maybe that's where I've been growing as a person through my own meditation practice and through relationships. Kalima, I love what you said about relationships—it's not about safety, especially intimate relationships. It's about how do you deal with those times when you're feeling unsafe? How do you still stay intimate with somebody? I'm realizing I think as I grow up, it's about being present.

In the past, if I had to do something like this meeting, I would have been feeling so anxious. I had to prepare. I had to look like I'm all competent, this and that as opposed to who cares? It'll just come up in the moment. At the same time, I had to do some preparation for today. Otherwise, I would have felt irresponsible.

Listening to you, Linda, talk about your experience makes me realize how as an Indian man I don't have to actually experience that. At least, I don't feel it. I may feel a certain vulnerability just because of people questioning, "What are you about?" It never to me feels like it's related to my race or skin color. I don't know what it is they project onto me being a man but definitely this is why this whole person-of-color thing is hard for me to ... Because the phrase "person of color," we're both people of color. Our experiences of being people of color are so different. I don't know. Do you identify as a—?

Linda: Blatina. (*mild laughter*) A black Latina.

Mohan: A Blatina. You're a Blatina, and I identify as East Indian. I don't think I have ever in my life experienced feeling like I'm being questioned for my competence because of my ethnicity. In fact, it's the opposite. There's associations made with Indian people being engineers and doctors and all this. I'm realizing that I don't face that walking into a classroom. I face my own insecurities that I've imposed on myself. I think I do face the thing of wanting to diffuse authority. I think I relate to what you're talking about Steve, wanting to diffuse that. Not take away my authority because I never feel like I'm going to be equals with my students because that's not appropriate. We have different roles here. Diffusing authority, I love that phrase.

I'm realizing I don't have to go through what you go through, Linda. The other thing that came up is that I feel like you must be very comfortable with yourself to be able to use that as a tool.

Linda: I just realized that. I think I'm aware of, like most people who get perceived as "other," you're aware that you're getting perceived as "other." You're aware of a lot of that unspoken stuff, but I realize I do feel very confident about it. I actually feel like it's an important leverage point. Walking in, I'm going to upset the apple cart just because I walked in. It's like, "How fun. Let's go with this."

Kalima: I think the other piece about this self-disclosure, particularly around folks of color, is how do we not become roadkill? How do we not feel the need to disclose so much to help the learning process along that we become just roadkill?

Mohan: What do you mean by roadkill?

Kalima: Roadkill, people are just observing, observing, observing, wanting more, wanting more, wanting more. Sometimes, the relationship with the professor is the first intimate relationship they have had with a person of color. How does that not become exploitive on both sides?

Mohan: Like a specimen?

Kalima: Yeah. We're not in a mutual relationship per se. *(Mutual agreement from all.)*

As folks of color, we are always sort of navigating power and identity and the associations related to both our end and theirs. We are responsible for helping students try to figure out possibly conflicting and even unconscious emotions such as, "Oh, yeah. You are a person of color. You're my professor. You're maybe somebody I don't actually respect but I have to respect or should I respect?" You never know what's happening with them, and navigating that in a way that holds your authority even though you're not even buying into this idea of authority but having to hold power in a particular way for your safety and the safety of the class. In fact, navigating this all in an attempt to hold onto our sanity, which becomes a game of walking in circles.

Kalima: As a person of color in the academy, I am always aware of how delicate this work of navigating multiple realities, needs, expectations, and false narratives is. Those are some of the other spaces that I occupy.

There is a constant sense of urgency in understanding their feelings about me, for me, thoughts about me, feelings for me and mine about them and our work together—it's all so complicated. Sometimes, they can't yet figure it out, partly because being in an authentic relationship with a person of color in authority falls way out of their worldview and experience, and because the way I am performing authority—examining, critiquing, and sharing power—simply isn't something they are all prepared or willing to do. It's hard and scary to work outside the box, so they show up in particular ways that force me to again reconstruct how we will be with one another, despite the pain and disappointment in said interactions.

Recently, a white student submitted her paper late. In fact, several students turned in their papers late, a few without permission. There was a point where I had to check myself around what did I do to create the space where adults felt it was okay to behave this way. In six years of being in the academy, this is the first time in my history in this particular institution that this happened. I was forced to engage in serious reflection that left me feeling vulnerable. Sadly, the very thing that I try hard to create in my classrooms, humanity, understanding, power-sharing, mutual respect, felt under review. It was a painful process because so much of who I am was challenged, which, of course, includes my blackness. I wondered if centering this level of humanity was wrong, that creating a class

Box 3: When Race, Power, and Humanity Collide

What does it mean when students request or expect a level of understanding or flexibility from the professor's role as an authority? What does this imply? What role does the professor's race play in this? Does the professor who expresses his/her humanity in class inadvertently "invite" a testing of his/her authority? How can a late paper sometimes serve as a litmus test of the professor/student dynamic/level of respect in the classroom? These are questions worth considering.

In connection with the discussion of the "late paper," situations that may touch on some of the themes raised in the above questions can include:

- The student explains he/she/they will be late for class and describes her/his/their challenge/situation in great detail and with confidence that you of course "get" it and understand.
- The student does not ask you to serve as a reference but then you receive a call or an email requesting that you serve as a reference.
- The student requests appointments for one-on-one meetings with you to ask you to advise him/her/them in ways that are not your job (career issues, family issues, etc.) because he/she/they

where I prioritized our full selves somehow sent a message of lower expectations or that within this politic was opportunity to take advantage.

That is so intimately caught up in my blackness because either you're taking advantage of me because you don't respect me, or you're taking advantage of me because you know I'm so down for the people, because I'm for the people, about the people, and about this work. I'm not even bought into the institution of power and the legacies of power that come with being in an institution, in an academy. What exactly is happening? It was all so murky. I really tried to work through it all—to live in my ethics, to live in my values. I went through an exhaustive and exhausting process with this student, so much so that my colleagues advised me to stop. In the end, I had to make a decision that aligned with those values, and I had to face a hard truth about what it means to share power through self-disclosure with folks who insist—whether consciously or subconsciously—in operating from a place of internalized racial superiority.

Self-disclosure, power sharing, mutual respect—all the conditions I value also expose me to folks who are not accustomed to that relationship to mess up in big, big, big ways. This is all caught up in identity as folks of color. The late paper is not just about irresponsibility—it's definitely all about identity. (See Side Box 3.)

Steve: Both of you are saying something that is so important for white faculty to understand: That there's so many more permutations of issues that people of color as faculty have to go through just walking into the room. Unless one is very conscious about power and authority, we have to accept this other reality in a deep and profound way where it's also part of our life work, too. It's not something that a new junior faculty member who is white is going to be aware of. They're caught up in their own immediate issues. *What do I have to do to be successful? What do I have to do to be good? Blah, blah, blah.* This awareness that they have colleagues of color who are going to go through something that they don't have to go through in addition to the demands to be a successful academic is something that I think would be a really good conversation for senior faculty to foster.

We senior white faculty have to take responsibility for fostering that conversation because we all know, for example, that the national data show that women of color faculty are rated a half point down on a 4-point scale on their academic abilities by students.

Call it whatever you want—implicit bias, discrimination, oppression—let's check off "all of the above." Each school and each

is "more comfortable with you."

Box 3: (*continued*)

There sometimes exists an unspoken expectation that standards will be ignored or modified due to a common social identity or the presence of an authentic relationship. Suggestions for handling the "late paper" and similar hurdles include:

- If a paper is going to be much later, the instructor might add on extra parts to the assignment, explaining it as a fairness issue to other students who were constrained by the tighter time frame.
- If there is any indication that a late paper or other performance issue is a result of issues of power, privilege, or feelings of inferiority, swiftly address it with compassion, clarity, and clear boundaries.

faculty has to look into this, that there are added questions and issues that people have to prepare themselves for. Some of the story you have to consider, and then this thing about self-disclosure can mean something very different for each person. This really needs to be understood. Understanding that calibration between preparing for academic excellence and revealing one's humanity and vulnerability, it's going to be different for us all. It has to be respected that it better be different for a number of people, especially people of color, that these conversations begin to turn these rating issues around.

The complexity of our students shows up in and out of the classroom. What we mean by complexity is too many of them show up unconsciously expecting what you said, Linda. Kalima, you were saying it, too, that people are going think so many different things. What did you say, the affirmative action wagon that you fell off? That all those doubts are immediately there. I never ever, ever, ever had to frame issues that way when I entered the classroom.

Linda: I'm aware of something that Kalima said that brought up a lot for me. I'm Linda. You're Kalima and all that that means in the world. Like you, I'm also representing every brown-skinned woman, every black woman, every Latina woman. If you disrespect me as those things in this room, I can't let that go unaddressed because I have to carry the work forward. I feel a responsibility to everyone else who's in that role, all of those like me at my institution. It's really important.

Kalima: You just made me think about *Pedagogy of the Oppressed*. Paulo says that "the oppressed will be the people who liberate the oppressors." I entered the academy with that as one of my foundational principles. Despite my critique of it on any given Tuesday, I still feel value in knowing that one of my daily charges is to not assume the posture of the oppressor and instead, act in ways that say I am free—I am whole.

Going into the academy, I resolved not to buy into the ways power is exercised. I mean really not wanting to buy into the academic expectations of "how to be." For black women, politics of respectability—how to dress, what to say, how to act—I simply do not want to play that game. The truth is, I can't afford to. Audre Lorde said we were never meant to survive, so I'm really reaching to model the way in which I want to live in the world—free, self-determined—and what that demands from me to be a little bit different. Self-disclosure is part of that difference. It just leaves folks of color so open all the time.

Mohan: I want to add to the conversation. It doesn't necessarily have to do with race but in terms of the authenticity of self-disclosure. I think I had the second class of my undergraduate LGBTQ elective. Every time I teach this class, I have this struggle. Do I come out in the first class? I read an article once written by an LGBTQ social work professor who says that if you don't come out, then you're contributing to all the oppression and internalized homophobia. I'm realizing he had a certain agenda there. My therapist helped me realize that. He said, "So why come out? What educational purpose is that serving?" Then I realized it was coming from my own anxiety. Then I realized that when the moment comes, if it comes, then I'll come out, and it came up in the second class.

After I came out to my students, then I talked to them about my fear about coming out. Not so much about fearing people's responses to me like homophobia or whatever. That's not what I fear. I'm very comfortable being gay and especially being gay in the classroom. I didn't want to feel like students were going to censor themselves about gay people or their own attitudes. One of my colleagues said to me, "Why don't you tell the students that? Why don't you tell them that you really encourage them to not feel like they have to somehow change what they say or think just because they have a gay professor?"

Something you said, Kalima, now about accountability or I think maybe Linda you said it: There is a certain pressure I feel teaching this class. I think it has to do with identity. I feel especially towards the LGBTQ students who are in that room, something that I feel, what is it? My colleague related it to being a black woman as a professor. She calls it an over-sense of responsibility. The way she said it, I realized that's what I'm feeling. I'm feeling a sense of responsibility in this class that's beyond anything else. Yes, I feel a responsibility to all of my students, but there's a certain protective-ness. It's almost like, "Oh, my gosh. Those LGBTQ students are looking at me to model something." I'm just putting that out there even though it doesn't have to do with race. To me, it is about the self-disclosure, authenticity piece and about feeling this over-sense of responsibility.

Steve: I think that what all of you are saying is so important because if white faculty don't see how many people of color and LGBTQ folks carry that responsibility and if we don't pick it up as well so that those issues get raised about how people get rated, how faculty of color get evaluated, we're perpetuating marginality. If we don't raise what implicit bias is, if we don't share the issue of vulnerability and how it plays out differently, how it's constructed differently for some people in authority than it is for others, we're allowing discrimination and oppression to occur. Our excuse is we have to cover all this important "substantive" material. We, therefore, leave our colleagues who are people of color or LGBTQ to handle the social issues and implicit bias issues that come up because you all simply walked into the classroom. If we senior faculty don't take these issues up consistently, we leave you out there high and dry because it's not going to go away for you.

I do have the privilege of letting these issues fall away from me, unless I opt into something else. If you opt in differently, then it's content for all of us. If we're going to make a learning environment for all, we have to see we do this for our own humanity and not just yours. Otherwise, given what's happening now with Black Lives Matter, for example, will move from an exciting focus today to irrelevance in a few years all over again. Without this attention from senior white faculty, in my 40-year experience, these issues of race and intersectionality will come up every five or eight years in an explosive way, and then they will go away. At some point, this kind of conversation needs to be sustained.

It will only be sustained if the burden of this is not simply on the few but is on everyone. It's what it's turned into, as you said, Linda, if it becomes an opportunity as opposed to any burden that only a few have to carry.

Linda: I feel like I would like us to say whose responsibility we think it is to raise these issues. We were going to tackle that later, but I don't know if we need to go in order. I feel like we should jump to that now because it feels logical in terms of what we're talking about now, so can we discuss whose responsibility is it to raise these issues?

Steve: Good. That's another question people have raised that we want to discuss.

Guiding Principles and Strategies

As with the previous conversation, students and faculty come into the classroom with expectations based on social identities, both spoken and unspoken, conscious and unconscious, about who is or isn't capable of teaching well. By layering in social awareness of this reality from the beginning, we begin to remove implicit bias that otherwise will be present in classrooms where faculty of color and open LGBTQ faculty are teaching.

- Principle: Disclosing obvious social identities is the responsibility of all faculty so that it begins the process of diminishing any implicit bias directed at younger faculty of color and open LGBTQ faculty.
- Strategy: Make sure all faculty meetings (including work groups) include an agenda item to help colleagues learn how to discuss social-identity issues in a thoughtful and planned manner that sets limits on disclosure but makes apparent an explicit expectation that social differences are to be appreciated and valued.

Disclosure happens as soon as people of color and those who are openly LGBTQ enter a classroom in ways that white, straight faculty do not experience, making boundary issues immediately more charged for them. Given dominant societal norms, some students will be testing levels of academic competence, intelligence, and readiness that are an added burden that white faculty often are not aware of that are at play for many of their colleagues.

- Principle: In pursuit of academic excellence for all, it is the responsibility of all faculty (especially those with tenure) to openly recognize these differences in how students may measure academic ability of their colleagues and to take steps to correct these implicit and explicit biases.
- Strategy: Make it a school- and program-wide expectation that all faculty will engage in a consistent discussion of social issues within their curricula and classroom, especially as it relates to interpretations of performance. Such a focus should be identified as of value for all faculty, and not as an added service to faculty of color and LGBTQ staff.

Self-disclosure must be an intentional and well thought-out decision. Often, in an effort to practice our ethics, folks of color and those from systemically marginalized identities bear the brunt of the risks associated with transparency whether that is objectification or unprotected overexposure. Some faculty who know the intimate details of invisibility feel a moral sense of responsibility to disclose. While self-disclosure is a worthy form of teaching and modeling, if done without reflection, it can also be a tool for self and community harm.

- Principle: Self-protection and intentional boundary setting is OK. Folks from marginalized identities must be supported and even guided in figuring out how much of themselves are safe and fair to disclose.
- Strategy: Faculty should commit a considerable amount of time assessing the readiness of their classrooms and themselves to handle self-disclosure. Faculty, particularly systemically marginalized faculty, must be internally aware and clear about what parts of themselves are off limits to include, as those areas that are easily triggered can also serve as unintentional disclosure.

CONVERSATION THREE

Question: "Is there really an 'Invisible Workload' that faculty of color and their LGBTQ colleagues carry that straight, white faculty don't?"

Background to this conversation:
This conversation emanates from the ongoing quiet conversations and concerns of faculty of color and LGBTQ colleagues that there are added, unseen hours to their workload as they meet with multiple students of similar social identities struggling to negotiate the larger academic environment. This added responsibility is one many speak about with ambivalence, both desiring to be supportive and yet concerned about the lost hours for research, self-care, and classroom preparation that most other faculty do not contend with.

Observations and Reflections:
- *This reality is mostly unknown and undiscussed in discussions of performance within most academic circles. What steps can be taken both by academic administration and senior faculty, especially those who are white, to ensure that over time this burden is acknowledged and supported?*
- *There is great stress on all areas of performance for junior faculty seeking promotion and tenure. At the same time, it is clear that an unfair advantage accrues for white faculty in critical areas of performance. What can be done to address this imbalance?*
- *Students of color come to faculty of color with particular needs and expectations stemming from individual and systemic racism, bias, and microaggressions both within and outside academic settings. Faculty of color often feel additional responsibilities for supporting students of color. To what extent do these responsibilities create additional rewards and burdens for faculty? In what ways does this reality apply to LGBTQ faculty and LGBTQ students?*

THE CONVERSATION

Linda: It's such a huge responsibility to bring attention and awareness to this issue, to grapple with the kinds of questions we're discussing here. *"Is there really an 'Invisible Workload' that faculty of color and their LGBTQ colleagues carry that straight, white faculty don't?"* How do we educate around these issues? It's certainly not in our job description. There are added issues that impact our performance as well that are mostly unknown in the school. For example, all faculty may have a certain number of students we have to advise, but I've got a separate, additional caseload of students of color who have picked me to talk to because they know intuitively or they assume that I must understand their experience of walking around with that double consciousness. They assume that I know that. They're seeking, what was the term you used, Kalima? I'm seeking—

Kalima: Common ground.

Linda: Common ground. I'm seeking common ground with someone. They come looking for us. The students come looking for us, and other professors of color that I've talked to have had this experience as well. The students come basically saying, "This is what I experienced in the classroom. This is the microaggression that happened to me. I am just devastated. I am exhausted. I just needed a safe place where I can say, even though I don't mean it, that I want to punch somebody in the face." But this is not in my job description and won't be part of any evaluation. I'm not getting a course reduction or workload reduction for this no matter how much of this I may do. I feel like it ends up being our responsibility. I don't feel like I can say it's not my job. It feels like a personal responsibility as a person of color. I can't walk away from that. There's my explicit job description, and then there's my implicit job description.

Mohan: Where I teach, definitely in terms of students, in fact, it's mostly students of color. If you're a white student, you're definitely in the minority. In terms of faculty we have in our department, it's still a majority white faculty, but we've got a good number of faculty of color. I think this whole question about added responsibility is an interesting one about why is it falling on certain people? I think maybe there's an assumption that white people don't have a race or white people don't have a color. I have a colleague who doesn't like the phrase "person of color" and says everybody has color. I think I understand that what's behind that is that we're all responsible because we have a skin color, and that skin color has meaning in our society.

"Microaggressions are the everyday verbal, nonverbal, and environmental slights, snubs, or insults, whether intentional or unintentional, which communicate hostile, derogatory, or negative messages to target persons based solely upon their marginalized group membership."
— Derald Wing Sue, Ph.D.

Steve: Do you feel that responsibility related to LGBTQ issues?

Mohan: Raising awareness about it or challenging?

Steve: Maybe other LGBTQ students coming to you a little bit more?

Mohan: Yes. I want them to know that they have a gay professor. My students just submitted these essays to me last week. I asked them to read one of Audre Lorde's speeches, "The Transformation of Silence into Language and Action." It's a beautiful three-page essay. It's actually given as a speech. I ask them to do a reflection piece about it. How does it resonate for them? When I read through their essays the first time, the personal experiences some of the LGBTQ students have shared in those essays, I guess I feel a certain protectiveness. Not that non-LGBTQ faculty wouldn't. I'm not trying to protect them from other people. It's very easy to talk about LGBTQ issues or sexuality in our department. I don't feel like that, but I do feel that now that they know I'm gay, maybe they will share. I feel a responsibility to all my students.

But I would imagine that my LGBTQ students would share things with me that they may not share if they didn't know I was gay. When I'm reading some of the things that they're writing about their experiences being gay in the world, I could relate. I can relate to that. I guess the responsibility comes from—you used the word "parental" earlier. I do feel a bit parental in that sense. I'm okay with that because I feel like I play that role, but I don't feel alone in that. I don't feel like, "Oh, my gosh. It's all falling on me." The environment I'm in, I feel like there's openness to talk about all this. I don't feel it's being dumped on any one person.

Kalima: I want to come back to the state of folks of color and women of color being rated half a point less, you said in our previous conversation?

Steve: A half point on a scale of 4.

Kalima: Out of 4, less than their white colleagues.

Mohan: That's big.

Kalima: That's big. I want to say, this idea of responsibility, it pisses me off because in some institutions, it's left completely up to the professor of color to include those readings. Those Audre Lorde readings on the syllabus were most likely included by a person of color. Once a conscious person of color enters the academy and is given academic freedom, academic content almost always changes.

All of a sudden, the professors of color willing to take the risk of including more reflective and diverse readings begin to look different from who has previously been there. The contours of folks' very being begin to shift. You can tell who's committed to the work because they're going to have Malcolm X, Audre Lorde, bell hooks, Mia McKenzie, Melissa Harris-Perry sprinkled throughout the syllabus.

I think that that is so grossly unfair. To further complicate this—this being the burden of professors of color having to include authors of color—let's consider the lesser-known, non-academic geniuses. Some of the lesser-known thought-producers aren't considered academic enough and therefore, once again, this leaves me open to critique. I think the inclusion of varied voices and politics should fall squarely on the institution. Institutions must make an explicit commitment to anti-racism, anti-oppressive social work practice.

I have worked in three institutions that have expanded my vision of what this commitment could look like and given me hope of what is possible.

One institution has a 20-year history of being committed to social work practice rooted in a commitment to anti-racism. Every one of their syllabi, almost every reading, is about identity and about why identity is central to the work. The syllabus is standard—subtractions are not allowed. Now, some would argue this comes at a cost to academic creativity. However, what this says is that critical race theory as it relates to clinical practice is valued and will be centered in the curriculum, and it will not be left up to professors to bear the burden of including it, nor will they be exposed to criticisms for teaching it. In fact, we're mandating that they do.

What we rarely ever see are readings focused on social workers of color working with folks of color. This institution provided those readings—again, lifting the burden of finding relevant and timely readings that address this topic and lifting the burden of finding and including said readings off the shoulders of folks committed to this work.

Now to be fair, they're not perfect. Sometimes the on-the-ground stuff isn't in total alignment with the rhetoric and teachings of those same readings, and students of color bear the burden of the implications as well as to demand change.

Mohan: What's that? The ground stuff?

Kalima: On the ground, the faculty stuff that happens. It hasn't been in alignment. However, the fact that this student body is so politicized is directly and partially a result of the curriculum.

The other institution, as a result of student-led activism, created a practice lab rooted in anti-racism. I want to say anti-racism because we want to think about this as an institutional issue. When an institution says that you have to practice, we have to teach from this lens, the sole purpose of this class is to teach from this lens, it sends a message. It makes it less about the personal agenda of the facilitator and more about the mandates of a larger system. It doesn't become our responsibility. We are backed up by an institution that says, "Yes. She's committed to it individually and personally. She's doubly committed to it institutionally." You can't even be here if you're not willing to be able to have these conversations or to engage in this real way.

If you have an issue, take it up with the dean. It is less likely that students will rise up against the system teaching liberatory pedagogy than if it were one lone professor. Another example is a dean paying for faculty and students to attend outside training with the People's

Institute for Survival and Beyond—The Undoing Racism Workshop. I remember being one of the students to organize for access to this training. I also remember an interim dean sending faculty through the training. We will never know the details around this decision; what we do know is that it has never happened again. The point is, that's commitment. Another NYC former dean of a school of social work paid every year for her students to attend the training. This is putting your money where your mouth is and showing you're more than words—you're about action, granting access, and not putting the burden on folks who have less power.

None of this should be special; this work is part of our ethics. We can go into the code of ethics and say the social workers are supposed to be dealing with issues of oppression and social justice, except these schools stand above the rest in that they are committed to doing this work in explicit and concrete ways. A lot of the schools want to say that they are dealing with that but are not on the ground actually dealing with that.

I think it really does have to come from the institution to protect the folks who are committed to it. There are white folks in the institution who are committed to it, yet may have way less to lose. The truth is, some have more protective factors than the folks of color do in terms of shielding against any hit they may sustain as a result of engaging in critical race theory. They may get one bad evaluation but really and truly probably published ten more times than colleagues of color, or if they're adjuncts, this is not their primary source of income or their primary identity. There's so many things that protect them, so if they get hit, they are protected. Some also get social capital in ways that folks of color don't get—institutional social capital.

Again, folks of color are more likely to receive social capital with the students but not institutional social capital. I really feel these institutions need to take more of a lead to protect folks of color who are actually doing the work.

Linda: It's double the identity but it's double the risk, too. The part of your identity that says, I am obligated to advance these issues, you can't let that go anymore. You do it, but you do it knowing that you're assuming additional risk.

You're already starting off with your half star gone. There's the additional risk. The only way to mitigate that, you're right, is that the institution really embraces this issue. I don't mean that it's just given lip service, like it says all the right things on the website or that the institution wraps itself in an anti-racist flag but that you really …

Mohan: Through actions.

Linda: … have built it in. I think there are many institutions where that's not happening, where it's just on the website. We're committed to this, but pretty much, the way it works on the ground is hopefully the professors of color will take it on themselves.

Steve: What I've seen in 40 years is that approach continues to be the far more dominant way that schools deal with racism issues. Even at my school, even though we have the required course with an anti-oppression lens, full-time faculty avoid teaching that course. At this moment in time, there are 18 faculty teaching the course, and only three of us are full time. The three of us have done it forever.

Mohan: All the rest are—everybody else is an adjunct?

Steve: All the rest are adjuncts. The adjuncts are spectacular, so the course goes well. The issue that emerges, full-time people are told that this course is very demanding. People are told that because the course is hard; if you really want to publish, you may not want to do this course.

Mohan: It takes a lot of time to teach it.

Steve: What it does is it requires an emotional as well as an intellectual commitment that you're going to work all the time. As a white guy, I say "choose your poison." I want to do this work and be free as opposed to where I was when I was 18 or 20. I didn't know anything as a young man. I was scared. I was afraid of this or that "different" person. Of course, I didn't know I was afraid. It becomes normative to have fear. It becomes normative to be nervous. It becomes normative to be uncomfortable where one gets anxious dealing with these issues. I don't have any of that terribly normative anxiety any more in my life. Yes, I do have more work in the actual course. I do have more work in my life where I'm always checking myself and being aware of these things that we're discussing. The truth is, I don't check myself anymore. I'm just aware it's who I am at this point. It was a gradual process. I didn't know why or where I was at 28. I had to go to work. I came to learn that this kind of work will set me free.

What white faculty have to realize is the norm of isolation, fear, being scared, being uncomfortable, being uncertain as to what to do about race and racism and other isms while seemingly being very substantive is a precarious way to build a career. How substantive can your work be that as soon as a student of color or an openly LGBTQ student raises a powerful question, you get thrown for a loop? It's been an awfully narrow corridor to walk one's career down if fear and trembling happens from an honest question or two. The other career avenue is that you integrate these issues into your work and your curriculum and your career and your life. It's a little slower and a lot freer. That's a choice people have to make. Freire has said that only the oppressed can free both the oppressor and themselves from our mutual dehumanization. I believe that to be true. By that, I don't mean that all people of color on the faculty are walking around acting oppressed.

I mean that there are stories from my life that help me understand what I have to do in order to be as free as I hope to be with other people and together engage in our mutual discovery of what it is for us all to see each other and experience ourselves as human. As you can tell by the way I speak about this, it's very emotional for me. It's very intense. I wouldn't have it any other way. There is frustration in me in that I don't understand why so few white people take up this approach to work and life. I really do believe this is the way to live a full life as opposed to some other way. Yet the other way continues to have so much more short-term, immediate benefit. It's easier to get that grant. It's easier to be pleased with that narrow approach with all its underlying discomfort and fear, but 30 years later, I don't think that's going to be true.

As people reflect on this, people who read this particular conversation, I think the issue of how we choose to live our lives—that there's going to be pain in whatever choice we make and the struggle we choose to live with. I choose, and I think all of us are saying we choose, the side of how to be free. I feel safe because I do this kind of work. I wouldn't feel safe about hiding from this.

Mohan: What you were talking about earlier about feeling integrated, having that as an aspiration, is interesting because as you're all talking about institutions, I'm just thinking about the institution I work for. Like I said, it's

United Nations in my classroom. It really is. Easily, there must be ten countries in the room. Our previous college president is a Latino man, and they just hired the third president. He's also a Latino man. It's interesting because we have an institution where you see people of color in the student body, in the administrative body, in the faculty.

It just made me think about having an anti-racism focus within an institution like that, which already has a very strong mission about serving communities in the Bronx. It's there in the mission, but at the same time, though, it does make me think about this whole thing of who's responsible around race? Not having it be just one faculty's decision to include this reading or that reading, but having that commitment institutionally basically says, "Okay. We are all creating this together." One of you said, I think, Linda, you said, in the earlier response about how we recreate the dynamics of society in the classroom. One idea, in addition to the safety thing, I've been very interested in is this whole notion of silence. Playing around with the word silence, being silent, silencing ourselves, choosing silence.

It came up in my research with gay fathers and about who has the power to ask other people questions about them? Who claims the power to say, "I'm going to interrogate you about who you are"? You walk into the classroom, and there's almost an implicit power that a student may be exerting to question your competence. Then you're in that position of maybe having to make a decision about, do I have to justify myself? I think this whole thing of having it come from an institution says, "Look, let's look at who does claim that power. Who remains silent about race? Who's able to go through the world not thinking in terms of race?" Although I have to say, all this stuff about race makes me realize how I've not dealt with race inside me so much. I'm much more focused about sexuality.

Steve: We're all learning about "what I didn't know what I didn't know." That light goes off for everybody at some point—white people on race, straight people on LGBTQ issues, people of color on pronouns like "they" for transgender folks. Nobody's perfect; we're all incomplete!

Linda: I want to share an image that's been going through my mind. I keep seeing this picture since we've been talking about this last question: It's a portrait of a black man's arm pulling up another black person by the arm. The image I keep having is of that effort of pulling someone up but with a foot on your back.

That's what I feel about this responsibility because I couldn't be more committed to that. Given this question about the invisible workload, I'm also incredibly aware of the presence of that foot on my back, and yet I recognize that I'm not even the most threatening of people of color. If I were a black male, it would be a whole other thing.

Kalima: For all of us, it's the foot on your back. Do you all feel scared to let them down, too? The students of color, the LGBTQ students?

Mohan: Yes.

Kalima: When something crazy happens in the outside world, this sense of responsibility to bring it into your classroom when you know other people aren't bringing it into their classroom is crazy-making.

Linda: They're looking at you hoping you will. They're hoping you will do it because no one's touching it.

Mohan: Letting go of what the syllabus says, what you're supposed to be doing in class.

Kalima: It's risky because that's also going to show up on your evaluation. Can you imagine this past year (with the number of murders of black men and women by police)?

Mohan: How many times we had to do that.

Kalima: Just this semester in the Fall of 2016 alone how many times we've had to do that and then on top of that, having to manage your own feelings, our own trauma, our own everything to be able to show up for them and then answer questions. (See Side Box 4.) It sometimes feels like, "Oh, my gosh. I can't believe I have to answer this question." Watch the silence and listen to the heady responses by white students or the heady responses of some folks of color that aren't rooted in healing, justice, or any real analysis.

Linda: Sometimes you can sense some students just checking out, as though this isn't a real class because we're talking about "that stuff." That may interest some people, but I'm paying $60,000.

Box 4: The Invisible Workload

The "invisible workload" is an unspoken and unacknowledged responsibility people of color, LGBTQ people, and other marginalized groups face in their workplaces to 1) make visible and give voice to socially charged issues which often go unnamed, 2) to provide a safe haven for students and others who are feeling the enormous weight of these issues, and 3) the expectation and sometimes pressure for faculty of systemically marginalized groups to coordinate, support, sponsor, or attend events related to race, power, privilege, and oppression hosted by students of color and the institution.

This additional, invisible workload experienced especially by professors of color and openly LGBTQ faculty members is related to:

- Students' perceptions of these faculty as being more understanding of challenges related to race, more experienced in navigating these issues, and more invested in their success.
- The unspoken expectation that faculty of color and openly LGBTQ faculty will create space to discuss pressing issues in the 24-hour news cycle despite personal proximity to and impact of the issue that may be harm-

ful, triggering, or not of political interest.

Box 4: (*continued*)

- The understanding of a responsibility in supporting students of color so that they have a better chance at succeeding.
- Feeling a responsibility, and sometime pressure, to ensure that the experiences of LGBTQ people are reflected in curricula, readings, and faculty discussions.
- How we often feel the need to "pay it forward" as someone went the "extra mile" for us, or we know what it feels like not to have had that support, and we want to provide it.
- An interaction of our own issues and what the students expect us to provide.

In addition to the regular duties required of these professors, the invisible task list often includes:

- Advising and mentoring a number of students of color and LGBTQ students per semester on academics, career development, interactions with other faculty and staff; respond to microaggressions; connect students to external resources and opportunities; and provide references.

Be a supportive colleague by:
- Couching requests for partnership on other issues with care and respect for colleagues' added demands so that their potential declining to partner is respected and not cause for concern or additional stress.

Mohan: Give me the textbook stuff.

Steve: That's why the institution has to say we have a responsibility that no one can be silent. The choice of silence is a privilege that we have as an institution that we have to give up. That is the work. If we want to take this on, we can do our individualized work, but it's still just individualized work. It's not institutional.

Linda: With a hope that because you're a member of the faculty, you somehow can do something. Meanwhile, you're thinking, I have no tenure.

Kalima: I'm expendable.

Steve: This is great, painful, real stuff. Holy mackerel!

Guiding Principles and Strategies

The following phenomena are two sides of the same coin: the additional responsibility that is explicitly and implicitly placed on faculty of color to address issues of race and racism or LGBTQ faculty to raise issues of sexuality and gender. Furthermore, faculty of color and open LGBTQ faculty carry an added level of responsibility related to mentoring and supporting students of color and LGBTQ students in their programs. Helping them navigate classes and field experience where troubling issues of microaggressions and previous trauma occur and yet otherwise may go unexamined presents an additional and unrecognized workload. Such added work can increase the pressure on these faculty members' performance as they carry the added weight of students' hurts, fears, and concerns that remain out of sight within the larger institution.

- Principle: It is the responsibility of all faculty to address both real and perceived microaggressions in the classroom and in the field so that all students come to recognize they are not being marginalized and that their concerns are not being slighted.
- Strategy: Schools and programs must formally engage in this frank discussion of the "invisible workload" carried by faculty of color and open LGBTQ faculty and take steps to begin dismantling the practices that make such an additional workload necessary. We need to all agree to share this risk of acknowledging and addressing the very real experiences of race and racism in the classroom so that the responsibility does not fall on the shoulders of a few.

Individuals, departments, and institutions may claim the power to remain silent on race and racism. Individual silence and institutional silence reinforce one another. We all have the responsibility to break this silence and doing so involves taking risks. Content on race and racism as well as issues of gender and sexuality must appear in all course content and not just on the syllabi of "minority" faculty. Otherwise, such content is perceived as an add-on to the "real work," thus opening up these faculty to lowered ratings and being perceived as less rigorous or less professional.

- Principle: Content on racism and homophobia/heterosexism as well as specific race and LGBTQ content must be seen as core content in all courses and not add-ons. When an institution teaches and practices through the lens committed to anti-racist and anti-oppressive social work practice, this has consequences for white, straight faculty, faculty of color, and LGBTQ faculty.

- Strategy: Curriculum committees in schools and programs should systematically review race and LGBTQ-related content in all courses, including assignments, with the expressed objective of guaranteeing such content is not treated as secondary to professional development.
- Principle: Both white people and people of color often feel isolated when they are confronted with the realities of race and racism in their academic relationships.
- Strategy: We need to help each other to break the norm of isolation that surrounds thinking and talking about race and racism. We can connect with each other around our fear and pain; we need not be alone. In particular, white faculty who have committed to this work can support other white faculty who are feeling scared and apprehensive to do so.

CONVERSATION FOUR

Question: How do we create a school environment that consistently engages its community in these conversations?

Background to this conversation:
While almost all schools and programs of social work have mission statements and stated commitments to the NASW Code of Ethics, many faculty committed to these issues experience discomfort in raising the issues discussed here—that they appear either dogmatic or "obsessed" with a particular social issue or issues. The desire behind this question is to see these topics of race, racism, LGBTQ issues and the like to be as normal to raise as any other curricular or field topic.

Observations and Reflections:
How do we break the vicious cycle of defensiveness from those seeking to raise these issues, and fear from those who hear them as a threat to where they locate themselves inside their academic institutions?

THE CONVERSATION

Mohan: We just had a pretty deep, emotionally charged conversation about some of the other questions, and it led us to reflect on the fact that we feel a level of trust with each other, that we can be open. I think, Linda, you brought up the question about maybe test driving what we're saying with some faculty to see if it actually resonates for them as useful. I think it leads to another question: *How do we create a school environment that consistently engages its community in these conversations?* If we look at the audience who's going to be reading this book, I would imagine it's mostly social work and some students. Is that the primary audience? And, maybe indirectly, agency professionals who adapt the questions to their teams?

Steve: Yes.

Mohan: In their work places—be it in the classroom, in a faculty meeting, or the lunchroom, or wherever they are—what is it that could help create the environment needed to have this level of conversation, and what gets in the way? Because I'm just wondering if faculty will pick up our book and say, "Well, that's a nice conversation; it was very interesting, but I can't see myself talking like that when I go back to work." I'm just curious what you all think about what is it that we're creating here and how can we create it out there, out there being in the workplace, and what gets in the way of it?

Steve: Well, I've had to struggle with this because there were, for years—given what happened earlier in my career as a young white professor really committed to anti-racism and social justice issues—instances when I raised a number of issues that almost cost me tenure, and so going back in to have these conversations later, as I did get tenure and I was promoted, I still found myself averse to addressing this with many people. I've really had to struggle to overcome that. It's almost like I would compartmentalize people where I would say, "Well I'm not going to talk to them about those issues because they're not going to really care or they're not going to get into it."

I've had to fight against that within myself because the fact is I've found that today more and more people are open. The key distinction for me is not what happens first when the topic is raised but what happens second. Because what happens first is, people may say something, as a younger faculty said, "I just don't know what to do." He said, "I teach a particular kind of course in research, and people will raise these issues like with Black Lives Matter, and I've never thought about that, and I'd like to be better."

For me, the hard stuff was I could say, "Well, gee, you've never thought about that. How come you've never thought about that?" Which is one question, right, that ends the rest of that conversation! Or I could say to myself, "Well, the guy at least is being open about trying to deal with this, so what can I do?" I have to do my own internal work, and then go back to him and say, "I hear what you're saying, and let's talk. Could you tell me in particular what happens that causes you to shut down?"

So my work was within myself first, where I learned to be open to his struggle, as opposed to condescending to him. He could then be honest and respond, "I just don't know what to say." What I then had to say was, "Well it's really great that you can be honest about having a struggle because from this we can begin to learn." Because I was once there, too. My earliest story in this work was many years ago, where I was thrown completely off by students who were in great pain together over racial issues, and I had no expectation that that was going to happen, and so I ended up almost throwing up in the classroom. That moment led me to interrogate myself for why was I sick, given that I was working in the South Bronx, I had as many black and brown friends as white, blah, blah, blah, and yet I was completely not equipped to handle students upset about racial differences.

So what I said 35 years later was, "It's okay to be in the struggle in that moment, to wonder what to do. What's not okay is to decide not to do anything." From there we've been able to talk. His response was, "What should I read?" I gave him some stuff on Elaine Pinderhughes because I think she's really terrific on helping white people understand both the intensity of what people of color go through and how whites really can't respond, or respond in the wrong kind of way, and it led to a really good conversation over time.

But there's something I need to underscore. I had to do an enormous amount of internal work to even want to go back in and talk to him. I am not equating myself with what others here have experienced, but too many years of being burned by other people in the past led me to be highly suspicious and actively indifferent to wanting to talk to people for a number of years at school, and that failure was on me because people changed. There were different people; it was a different experience. I had to really work on myself before I could do that because in other instances I wanted to find people wrong as much I wanted to find them open. Anti-racism superiority can be its own problem, too!

Kalima: This work is exhausting. I mean I don't want to always live my life in a space of sadness. Even when I think about my own workplace, I have a visceral reaction. I sometimes can't explain it because I both love and am deeply troubled by it all. I'll do my best and please tell me if you have experienced this.

I work in a public school of predominantly white, young, and interestingly bubbly teachers. I know it isn't the total picture. However, I look at white folks, and I'm like, "Wow, what does it feel like to be so light?" Not in complexion but sort of this levity that they have in the world because they're not necessarily burdened the way we are. They may care about it and feel passionate about it; however, they are rarely directly impacted by it. Their access to daily and ordinary joy seems to be uninhibited. Even as I am writing ten things I am grateful for in my gratitude journal, I'm thinking about Alfred Olango, whose mental illness was no fault of his own, and he was killed. Even through my smiles, I am thinking about the way the lives of people who look like me are explicitly made irrelevant.

All he did was hold the three-inch cigarette in the air. I'm thinking about his sister who called the police for help. She had to wait for an obscene amount of time to even be recognized, and once they finally responded, out of what seemed to be sheer annoyance, they did not take the time to troubleshoot with a mentally ill person. Instead, they killed him.

How does this happen? How do I experience that type of levity when I have the sorrow of my people heavy in my heart. The truth is, I don't get to go into work and feel that lightness. Even if I want to check out, I still can't check out, so I just look at white folks with their little rosy cheeks at times, and I'm like, "What does it feel like to be like that?"

It's so hard to enter into their spaces and feel normal or affirmed. There's no way to ignore the pain I feel and, at times, the hopelessness. There's no way to thwart the anger or ignore the chronic sadness. I actually don't want to; I don't want this environment to rob me of the humanity. I want to allow those feelings to exist without being overwhelmed by them.

Who wants to always be the Debbie Downer? I don't always want to be sad; I don't want tragedy to be our only point of entry into relating to one another. However, I have to be authentic if I am even going to attempt to be in conversation with folks, but before I am my full self, I've got to trust that you can even hold the conversation before I enter the conversation because once I enter, I'm way too vulnerable to be even thinking about how to educate you, get you to understand, hope that you have the right response. It's just way too much.

Then I look at those rosy cheeks, and smiling eyes and say, no. I think you're way too invested in this state of mind, and you deserve to be. It's much harder to engage authentically cross-racially. There has to be years and years of developed trust and proven commitment to racial justice and difficult conversations to allow for the depth of sharing that is inherent in genuine conversations. There's too much at risk, especially for folks of color who are feeling and experiencing the grief of our community.

Risk-taking in that I sometimes can never tell what the person is going to say or how they are going to respond, whether that is verbally or nonverbally. It makes sharing scary, and it feels like a dangerous space. For me, once I open up, I cannot take the risk of you responding from a benign place, yet completely off target, because at that moment, I realize that in order for us to continue to be in an authentic relationship, I have to figure out if I can and want to hold what just transpired.

I can definitely take a step back and yet, even that is something else I've got to hold. If I decide to stay, I've got to figure out how to respond, but as I am looking at the person, watching their realization of their impact on me, seeing their embarrassment, there is the heavy unspoken exchange because it all hurts so much, and then that person starts to feel guilty. I feel exhausted.

It's too much, and I sometimes need a space and want a space where I'm not forced to think about all the pain where I am not confronted by this seemingly untainted joy. I want a space where I don't have to actively think about or feel all the sadness; I need some kind of respite. The truth is, I'm thinking about it in my home. I'm thinking about it in my family, and when I'm on the train, and I see homeless folks on the train. I feel like I don't get a break, and so when I have those moments of looking at these jolly white folks, I'm like, "What is that?"

So I don't go this deep with them. However, I do find the pieces of me that I can expose to sort of work on behalf of the children, but it's exhausting. But again, to not have a space to be my complete 100% at work—where I spend almost half my day—is tough and another bit of sadness to contend with.

Linda: I'm gonna drink to that. *(Everyone laughs.)*

I feel you though. I feel you, and I agree I can't live like that. I just cannot live like that. My spiritual faith sustains me through a lot of that, and even in that, sometimes the race stuff has to creep in. My faith is very real for me. Sometimes I find myself thinking, "I hope I was not just fed a whole bunch of crap in an effort to just keep our folks down" kind of thing. You know, how religion was used to keep slaves under control. I'm just kind of like, "Okay, don't even go there. Don't let this source of strength for you be taken away by the fact that it was used by some as an oppressive tool."

Kalima: Linda, I wonder if you feel like this, too. Today, we were talking about this idea of collective shame. I asked a Dominican guy in my office, "When a Dominican acts up in the street, do you feel ashamed? Do you feel shame when that happens?" And he's like, "Well, uh ..." He did not have a definitive answer, which led me to wonder is it because he had never even thought of the concept of shame when his people act up or because he doesn't? I chose not to pursue it because I couldn't shoulder another moment of not being recognized, especially from a person of color.

I asked the black woman, and you already know what she said. Yes, she absolutely does feel shame. When something happens in the wider society, and it's a person of color, we're collectively like, "Shit."

Mohan: It happened to me in the rest stop in Delaware on Route 95 yesterday with this Indian couple, when they were ordering their drinks from Starbucks. They come from the same part of India that I come from. I felt all the embarrassment that I felt as a child and even as an adult about being brown, about being Indian, about being different, about eating with our hands.

There's a certain dissociation, I'm realizing, that I've allowed myself to do. I've allowed myself to dissociate from being brown. I've allowed myself to dissociate, and I've used my intellect, I've used my motivation and professional drive and the 10,000 graduate degrees I have, all of that, and then it's all compounded with being gay and everything.

What is this striving, striving, striving? I would use striving as a way in, a way to dissociate from all the shame of not wanting to even look at myself physically. So it came up for me yesterday in this rest stop watching this couple, but at least now I have a part of me that is aware of myself. "Oh, look at me being shameful about this couple." It's what I was talking about earlier about wanting to align myself, growing up with the message of we align ourselves with what people. We need to not be who we are, and then there's a double message, which is that we have to be who we are. It's crazy-making. I feel for my parents. They're the ones who had to go through this. They protected me, but they had to go through this as new immigrants to this country.

I'm glad you asked that question although it really took me down a path of thinking. So much for this one not being deep.

Linda: Nothing like light questions!

Mohan: I am fortunate that I have a workplace right now where I feel a certain authenticity. I'm able to be myself in a lot of ways. I don't talk like this with my colleagues, but I do talk with some of my colleagues about things like this, and they get it. I think there's something about the fact it matters to have people from different parts of the world, it matters to have different skin colors, it matters to have different races in a faculty. It really matters. It matters to have different sexual orientations. I don't feel alone at all.

So the conversations are happening, I believe. The word that comes up for me is intimacy. It's like in a relationship. We were talking about relationships last time. I loved what you said, Kalima, about relationships. It's about willing to just be in the fight because I think it requires the fight to figure out who you are in a relationship and to develop intimacy with each other. That's really hard; that level of intimacy is hard. I'm also thinking about boundaries. There's certain boundaries that get created, that maybe need to get created, in a workplace.

I think when you start opening up the door to these types of conversations, how do you not become intimate? I mean, look at this. I think any question we have now is going to go there in our conversations.

> **What does it mean to "develop intimacy" in the classroom?** *Intimacy is the courage to embrace our whole selves and the desire to connect to other human beings so that they can see our full humanity. Developing intimacy in the classroom means creating a space where students and teachers can allow their full selves to emerge in the learning process, and in so doing, connecting with our shared humanity.*

Guiding Principles and Strategies

Harkening back to the original question of this chapter, a vital ingredient for a group to become a community is intimacy. We begin to grow in intimacy by having difficult conversations with one another, and at the same time, we need to feel some level of intimacy in order to have these difficult conversations. In either case, the healing that comes from building intimacy and community requires each of us to take a risk and start somewhere!

- Principle: Academic and agency settings, like every other setting in America, will be experienced differently by everyone in that setting, with many people living with social difference as an identified "problem" that others have not recognized. This recognition must be respected and worked with as a normal, albeit painful, reality that cannot be overcome by ignoring it, wishing it away, or seeing the discomfort it creates as a problem made by the people living with such pain.
- Strategy: These issues of social difference over time can be constructed as healthy rather than harmful so that consistent, sustained application of new norms and expectations are woven into the classroom and field settings, allowing everyone to grow through an ongoing process of mutual discovery and awareness.

PART TWO:
THE CLASSROOM CONVERSATIONS

CONVERSATION FIVE

Question: *How can I create a healthy give-and-take between people in classrooms or agencies when there are social differences between us?*

Background to this conversation:
This conversation centers around issues of how to establish trust between people who may have differences in experience as well as differences in social identities, and dynamics of power are at play between students and faculty or agency staff.

Observations and Reflections:
How much closeness can we expect among people in a classroom or agency setting? Does this work require a high bar of personal intimacy to be successful?

THE CONVERSATION

Linda: I'll start here. Given the kind of disruption we're mentioning throughout our earlier conversations, are we saying that's the work? That you have to take the risk of getting intimate with people in these classroom and academic environments that you might not get intimate with?

Mohan: Well, that to me is the interesting question. Maybe people don't get into this because they think about the classroom construction. The classroom has been constructed as an intellectual environment. So, it's almost the way we create these dichotomies around intellect and feeling and body and all of that. Maybe as a faculty we don't allow ourselves to go there because we're not supposed to. We're supposed to keep it at a certain place, I don't know. Maybe these dichotomies serve to maintain social differences. The question is: *How can we create a healthy give-and-take between people in classrooms or agencies when there are social differences between us?*

Linda: I think we should support a principle, which is that you cannot do this work on an intellectual level only. We could say that as an explicit principle because it's just not possible to do this work only on an intellectual level. Now, we then have to grapple with if we go outside of the intellectual realm, how far do we go? Where's the boundary? Is there a boundary? But it can't stay in the intellectual realm only because if it does, then it really isn't being addressed.

Steve: Linda, let me ask you something about your relationship at your foster care agency Inwood House where you were the executive director. I mean this in terms of this relational, deep work with a white woman who was your number two because you two developed an extraordinarily close relationship that allowed both of you to be fully who you were, and at the same time, you're both different human beings.

What was it that happened—and I'm not talking about making either you or her look better than other people—that allowed you, and I know it certainly allowed her, to feel that you each could be fully who you were with the other, and at the same time, you still made sure the work got done?

Linda: I think the case study with Pat (the number two) was that she made an effort right off the bat to see me as a human being when we entered that agency workspace.

Steve: Yes, she had been the number two before you got there.

Linda: I feel like she operated with me based on the assumption that I was fully qualified to be the executive director, so she was more interested in knowing who I was as a human being, so, for one, I didn't have to prove that I was worthy to be in the position. We just were able to skip right past that. That was a given, and then we could get to know each other as human beings. I feel like that was key.

The other was she had a keen sense of the difference between what role you occupy in an organization and then who you are. She was real clear about her role in that organization and my role in that organization. Not conflicted at all about, "Well, maybe I kind of sort of want to be the executive director; I kind of sort of should be the executive director, but you're the ..." She was so clear, about that, and then she very concretely demonstrated this commitment to helping me to succeed.

Trust got established very quickly because of that, and I could be simultaneously vulnerable, like when I felt like I had no damn idea of what I was doing, and not be diminished by her in any way. That's very rare. It's very rare in a leadership position to be like, "I don't know anything at this moment about this," and still keep your credibility as the leader who's supposed to know everything.

That was very special; that was a way in which we bonded, and then from my perspective, I knew that she had a lot of knowledge about the organization and about the work, so I was able to both lean on her and tap that, and she gave it very freely, very willingly. Then we discovered we had very similar values about the work, and then a very similar sense of humor, and then we just took off, but I think it was that she was very clear. I remember her being very clear in the very early days, like, "Let me be clear; I don't want this job, so you're not walking into an organization where you have to wonder if your number twos really want your job because I couldn't be more clear."

Mohan: So Pat was already working there when you became executive?

Linda: She was one of the number twos; she was a deputy executive director.

Mohan: Okay, and then you were hired as executive director.

Steve: That says a lot, though. Everything you just said was exactly what we need in all our places of work and classrooms, which is that you can show up in your full humanity, you're not being tested, waiting for somebody to play "gotcha." That's not at play. It's assumed you're smart, as opposed to you having to prove you're smart, and then you get to be human, and then you get to be vulnerable, and then the other person has something they want to contribute but they want to learn from you. Everything we were talking about in an earlier conversation is removed from the equation, so now it's just, "Can we deal with each other and do the work?" and all that kind of stuff.

One of the things I know for myself, I've been thinking about this as people have been speaking: If there's no emotion within related to the topic at hand, if it's just an intellectual thing, like "Social justice is very important, but I don't know what it has to do with you and me." You know that kind of thing?

I have to know that people mean it when they talk about racial issues or LGBTQ issues, that this is for real and not an add-on to the work about race, about racism, about intersectionality, that the issues at hand are not the occasional, "Oh, I have to address that, too; I'll be happy to add that to my portfolio," but it's woven into who we are. While, of course, straight white people understand that they're not living an oppressed life, but they've crossed over, it's an existential moment that I had to face, and I think any white person has to face on many of these issues where you cross over existentially and say, "This is how I live my life," as opposed to, "I get to be holy" for a few hours a term.

The real thing that I've seen in child welfare is the workers who see that those kids are *their kids*. Whether they're black, brown, white, they do really well in the workplace. That kid's hurts are their own kids' hurts, and they get really upset about what's happening because it could be their child; then it's clear that they get it. Frankly, I'll tell you the truth, Pat has told me stories, and I've seen this as well, that overwhelmingly it's mostly white people who don't get this about the kids, but it's not a guarantee that every person of color is going to get it either or have the same commitment to those kids because they don't.

It's very freeing. There are no groups of perfect people out there, but the belief that this is part of your life forever on an emotional level—and that's just why I always have to learn more—that is the marker that allows me to say about a colleague, "I want to go back and talk to her. I want to go back and talk to him." That's the marker that I know means I'm willing to keep with the conversation. They're truly all our kids.

Of course, I also have to recognize that I never have the depth of pain or struggle that, Kalima, you mentioned, or all of you have mentioned in other ways.

Mohan: Also something you said, Linda, about when Steve and you were talking about bringing in that full humanity, being seen as a human being first. I have a question for you, because it sounds like it happened quickly or early; it wasn't something that you built over time. There was something that happened early, and that's what I find in the workplace. The people that I feel that with, it happens quickly; it hasn't built over time, and it doesn't happen with everybody, and it doesn't need to. Thankfully, I can say that I've got a good number of colleagues who I feel that with, and I think that's one of the reasons I love working there.

I'm just curious about that relationship back in your agency. What is that? She saw you as a human being, you saw her as a ... ? I would like you to say a little bit more about that. Then the other thing that I thought you said was really helpful was something about roles. You're able to be full human beings, and you preserved your professional roles and boundaries. That's maybe the fear people have—maybe it's a misperception— that if we do treat each other as full human beings, that our roles are going to all just wash away, and it's all going to become therapy, it's all going to become incestuous. It'll become unprofessional, right? But it sounds like you said, "So what? Now you have both."

Linda: I was her boss, and she respected me as her boss even though there were things that she knew more about and had more experience than I did. The glue here was that we knew that there was a destination that we both wanted to get to in the work. If we worked together, we could get there, right? It was this willingness to be vulnerable, transparent. "I know this, but on that issue, I don't know what I'm doing." Being able to do that and know that the person actually can see you fully enough and that doesn't diminish you. That makes you human, the fact that you don't know everything, but it doesn't diminish you. There's really no threat to your ego integrity because you know that they know that you're a full human being, and you know that they're a full human being.

That was the magic, but I do have a question for all of us. I think this is a challenge to what we're trying to do with this book and in this work. If it takes that special, whatever we're going to call it—chemistry, alignment—for this to happen, then why are we even doing this book? Because what does it mean, then, if people don't go there as a matter of course, or they like to stay in an intellectual realm? Then is there no hope?

Kalima: I think there is.

Linda: What are we saying then about the work? What are we encouraging people to do? Are we saying, "Look, take the risk of reflecting on some of these things yourself. Take the risk of engaging in a conversation with someone you might not engage in a conversation with on some of this"?

What are we really saying one needs to do?

Mohan: When the chemistry's not there. You don't have to rely on that chemistry.

Steve: It's interesting as you were talking about it, your relationship with your number two. I'm thinking back to this experience twenty years ago with this fellow professor, an African American among the clinical faculty to whom I wanted to speak and how he teared up when I asked him a substantive clinical question on transference and countertransference. He became so emotional because I didn't approach him first as an African American alone. Like you said, Linda, Pat approached you as a substantial person. It was assumed you had the ability to be ED. I think about this fellow who teared up because up to that point he had

had no experience of white colleagues approaching him as clinically smart about stuff unrelated to race.

I think one of the things is, if you're going to demonstrate that you care about the humanity of the people you're with in mixed, racial, cultural, multicultural company, don't approach that person simply about, "Well what do you have to say about race or sexuality or ..." all that stuff that you talk about so much, but approach him instead with, "What do you feel strategically about what we need to do?" What do you, Kalima, as an organizer or Mohan, in all your clinical brilliance, or maybe something about math and statistics, and you, Linda, as an executive, with your leadership skills. The racial or sexuality stuff may get factored in, it may not get factored in.

See the person across from you as the substantive person that you assume they see you as, they see me as, and then the other stuff can emerge. This is where white people like me have a lot of work to do. This is our work, not yours.

It's our responsibility to address it; it's not yours to have to raise it every single time, with that burden and that weight and that sadness that gets carried into it. If it's all on you, then there is no hope. But there is hope if we say, as Paulo Freire wrote, our own humanity is bound up in our relationship with the oppressed, recognizing not that we save them but the reverse—"that only the oppressed can save us from our mutual dehumanization." If we can't see that that's about us being freed, not by simply dwelling on these anti-oppression issues but by seeing the humanity of everyone, and then weaving in these other factors—to me, that weave in the midst of our mutual humanity is how transformation occurs.

Kalima: I just want to say one thing because I have a comrade at work; he is my tried-and-true comrade. He's a white, privileged man, and when I tell you privileged, I mean, he looks like Clark Kent. It doesn't matter where we go, folks are flocking to him, and he's incredibly smart, he's passionate, and he's political, but the thing that makes him my tried-and-true comrade is that he's willing to put himself on the line, and he never has to be asked to move to the front lines.

The truth is, he's still wrestling with his privilege and wrestling with his male privilege and his good-looking privilege and his class. He has every privilege there is, and he's still wrestling with it, but he's actually in the work, and he's willing to have the conversation. He is willing to say the things that I am thinking, and I'm like, "Oh, damn, should I say this, should I not say this?" All I have to do is just look over, we just look at each other, and it's communicated, and he will take the lead on it, or it's communicated, and I'm like, "I'll do it," and then he'll support.

I think, like one of the things you said, Steve, it's this willingness to be on the front lines. It's a commitment to using one's privilege to move work forward in a way only his compilation of attributes can facilitate. It's the ability to sit with me and allow me to be sad without needing or wanting to cheer me up. (See Side Box 5.)

I want to circle back to your experience, Linda. First of all, I think your number two was operating strictly from a feminist perspective, where competition is not part of our language. Feminist thought says that we do not operate within patriarchal ways and systems and ways of being, that your emotions are

Box 5: Willingness to Be on the Front Lines

A "willingness to be on the frontlines" related to the topics of this guide means being willing and able to strategically use your positions of power and privilege to step into and raise difficult conversations and topics that often appear in classrooms or faculty meetings—far easier with tenure, and yet always needed (perhaps away from more formal, public meetings).

bits of information; we honor the irrational. Patriarchy will say that it's our emotions, that we're being so irrational, but some women have a way of supporting one another in that irrationality, and it is okay because that is information, and we are collaborative, and we lift as we climb, and, whether folks call themselves feminist or not, if they are living in this way, they are.

I think that is a strictly feminist point of view and way of being in the world. I think that is so honorable, and so wonderful in the workplace because it can be people who are thinking that they're being anti-oppressive and operate strictly in a patriarchal setup.

With my tried-and-true comrade, he is doing the work, and he's reading, and he doesn't ask me certain questions; he just asks me, "What have you read?" He has read almost every one of my favorite books, and so we can have conversations. He does his own work, and then he sends me articles, and I think that is a person who is committed to the work, and then we get to the emotional part where I can just sit and cry, and he'll just sit in a space with me, or he'll sit and cry, and I'll sit in a space with him, and that's that. We just be.

Then there are other people in my workplace where we're not quite as tried-and-true in terms of intimacy, but we are comrades. We are on the same sheet of music. We know where we want to see this school go. We know how we're going to insert this conversation. We literally plan it out the way we want to see it, but we don't have the same level of intimacy. We have the same level of vulnerability, but not the same level of intimacy as my tried-and-true comrade.

Linda: I think Pat saw me, and I saw her. There's something very powerful, if we think about when we experience it, when we're seen. Like, "I see you." "I see you." Right? I want us to keep thinking about the implications for what we're challenging our readers to do or to try to do.

Kalima: And what is the formula?

Steve: We'll come back to that because we can't expect every-body to be tried-and-true comrades or to be a fighter for social justice day in and day out, but maybe that second category that you mentioned is possible.

Mohan: Vulnerability.

Steve: Having vulnerability based on a common commitment is something I think we can strive for, and on that note we can end. Good lord, this is intense!

Guiding Principles and Strategies

One of the key insights regarding the creation of "safe enough space" is not to seek perfectibility and political correctness from students or oneself but to embrace each person's ongoing self-discovery of how his or her own stories and experiences have shaped and constructed each person's perspectives on race, racism, LGBTQ issues, and all other social realities woven into a person's life. It is therefore lifelong work, cast and changed over time, for us all, not an "academic experience" to be shelved upon completion of a class or program.

- Principle: A safe-enough space or environment does not require all people to be mutually intimate with each other in order to be successful in creating such an environment. It does require people to demonstrate an active commitment to growth on understanding issues of social difference and the power inequities built into them.

- Strategy: Approach these issues with an open vulnerability that some things one will always need to learn from others.

  Be willing to express openly that you engage in these issues for your own well-being and not only for others.

- Principle: Safe work and classroom environments remain open and effective when people are approached with respect for the formal positions they hold and for their substantive talents both related and unrelated to their social identities.

- Strategy: Be conscious of demonstrating respect for the assumed authority a person holds in her/his position. At the same time, seek out his/her expertise on substantive issues that do and do not relate to his/her social identity (such as clinical, leadership, or strategic skills).

CONVERSATION SIX

Question (raised by white faculty): How can I teach about poverty to my students, many of whom have been impoverished, when I am middle class?

Background to this conversation:
Many faculty express unease about teaching material on oppressive conditions and historical discrimination that they themselves have not experienced, especially with students in the classroom who come from what seem to be difficult backgrounds.

Observations and Reflections:
No one expects a teacher of, say, Italian literature of the 17th century to be Italian (let alone be 400 years old). Why do so many faculty and students feel unable to be knowledgeable about important social and economic issues?

THE CONVERSATION

Steve: The question we're going to take is, *How can I teach about poverty to my students, many of whom have been impoverished, when I am middle class?* As the white member of our group, I think it's important that I start this one. I think that this is, in many ways, frankly, a kind of an avoidance of discomfort built into the question itself. I think it's our responsibility to teach that material.

If you follow the logic of this question, it would mean that nobody could teach anything except from their own identity, which of course would be an impossibility. Instead, the responsibility of a white faculty member is to make sure of two things. First, in this case, be sure of the data and the history they reveal that fully explains what poverty is all about, that it's not situated in individuals, but poverty stems primarily from structural and historical conditions.

Second, within those lectures, we take responsibility for making sure that the stories people have are also part of the narrative about poverty. We have to, because the data makes students understandably think about the level of victimization created by impoverished conditions. If you only work from the fact that people have been oppressed for generations and centuries, and out of that objectify poor people and people of color, it becomes problematic because they're only victims. Their stories matter that show something other than their misery.

Of course, all of this is intensified by race, gender, and sexuality. Therefore, it's also our job to explore that part of the historical narrative that includes stories of people's resilience and capacity to overcome those horrors. The practice of this as a white faculty member is to be able to be confident and clear on exploring the history of oppression well, and at the same time, making sure that voices of resilience and capacity are also part of what we discuss in the classroom.

Again, just as we've talked about earlier, this is about the ability to hold multiple truths. This ability to hold more than one reality here is important. (See Side Box 6.) I think that in today's world, we have to work at breaking through this idea of identity politics that is addressed to only one issue having legitimacy. My frank belief is that there's a primacy of race in terms of intensity and the length of oppression in America, and simultaneously, of course, there are issues of classism, of sexism, of homophobia that have to be addressed as well. That alone can be controversial. It's something

Box 6: How We Hold Multiple Truths

"Holding multiple truths" requires us to acknowledge two competing realities that seem to contradict each other, yet are both "true" at the same time. Some examples of this concept include:

- All parents in child welfare are due respect, and some parents put their children at risk.
- Many white people are financially strained and afraid, and never have to fear being stopped while driving, while financially successful people of color live with that fear each time they go for a drive.
- All poor folks, despite race, are subject to oppression, invisibility, and exploitation by larger systems, AND for folks with multiple subjugated identities, the consequences are sometimes lethal and committed with impunity.

that I think is very important to address. The practice that I make of this is to not create the hierarchy of oppression, or the Oppression Olympics that we've talked about before, and to instead examine the data related to what racial oppression has looked like in this country related to slavery on the one hand, genocide of the Native Americans, the stealing of the land of Latino Americans and the diminishment of their culture, alongside the economic struggles numbers of white people have had.

We've got to be able to draw the conclusions that, yes, many people have struggled in this country, *and* some people have suffered far, far more than others. That should not foster guilt. It shouldn't foster a sense of, "I can't be there. I can't be able to talk about it." In fact, what we have to be able to do is to talk about it critically while holding these multiple realities for our students.

Kalima: This is interesting because you started this conversation off as a person who identifies as white, and I want to start this conversation off as a person who identifies as Afro-Latina and a first generation American because I find that my experience of socioeconomic status, even though I'm a person of color, and I'm seen as black, may not be the same as other folks.

Sometimes there's a single story that we all have had a shared experience of poverty, even I should be able to talk about it. It's not even just because you're white that you think you shouldn't be able to talk about it, or this may be something that is only limited to white folks who may not have grown up poor. It's also that there are black folks who didn't actually grow up poor in the same ways that some of the folks in our classrooms have grown up or those who are still in that situation.

What I'm always trying to navigate is the ways in which

I know that I am seen in the classroom as a black person who does not have that narrative, yet some people may think that I should have that narrative or think that I may have that narrative, and I don't. Being able to hold the "both and" of not wanting to seem uppity in that space or patronizing because I just simply don't have that.

It's been interesting for me to navigate class. When students bring up places that they have traveled to, and I can say, "Oh, yeah, I've traveled there," how that becomes a gap between myself and other black folks because they may not have had those same experiences that I have had. I lived a life where I took vacations every year. Sometimes, the only way in which we know how to bond is over our subjugated identities rather than our privileged identities.

That's my space of struggle and contention and the ways in which I have to begin to navigate that. Even the things I say may seem insensitive. The other day, I was talking about self-care with my students, and I was telling them that there is nothing I wouldn't do to take care of myself. A student said to me, "That's class privilege," and I was like, "You're absolutely right." I'm not going to lie. I have class privilege that allows me to have access to self-care modalities, traditional or non-traditional, that other folks may not have.

How do I lay it down? It's complicated because I'm challenging what people may think, but I'm also challenging relationships and ways people relate to me. In talking about poverty, I also talk about how I came from an immigrant family, and in this immigrant family, we had to be incredibly resourceful, not only because some of us didn't know the language, but because we were completely new to this country, so we had to be resourceful in ways that other folks may not have had to be resourceful.

There's things in our community like susu where people pool their money, so economic status comes from that. From a shared commitment, to pooling your money, and then everybody grabs a hand. People have bought houses from that. People have traveled, sent their kids to college, all this kind of stuff. I have, and people even in my community have, operated underground markets. Lotto, we call it playing the numbers. People have been in the lotto system that comes from Panama and have been in that type of market as well.

I think hard about how to talk about poverty when I haven't experienced poverty in the traditional sense, yet understanding my parents were materially impoverished because they were immigrants. They didn't know how to use the system; they didn't know how to access resources; they didn't know how to do any of that. They were forced to figure out how to do that within our own community. Those are real material experiences, but me as a young person, I didn't feel it because my culture and community were resourceful.

If you didn't have food, you wouldn't even know your family wouldn't have food because the entire community would come together and fill that need. I think my experience of poverty also may be different from how other folks are experiencing it. I did not go without food, housing, medical care, or a good education. However, my parents did not fully know the system and often were clueless as to what existed and their own eligibility. Even today, in 2016, folks have so much access to see what other people have, so they're very clear about lack versus way back when you didn't have that level of awareness.

I think like what you said, it's holding the reality of the

"both and," that there are real, lived, material experiences of folks who are impoverished that impact education, housing, healthcare, policing, everything. There's also something very rich in some communities in the ways in which they try to survive. I don't want to romanticize it, but I think it's the holding toward the "both and" in our classroom discussions. The truth is, not all folks of color share the single story of poverty as we understand it. It's really important to create space for varied experiences of poverty but more so spaces for stories of resourcefulness and resilience. Using this framework has really allowed me to teach something I may not know everything about or know it as it is defined in America.

Mohan: I can relate to many things that you said, Kalima. There's so much in there. When I first started thinking about this question, I thought, "I'm coming at it from a standpoint of being a middle-class Indian man who grew up in the U.S. since he was one, whose parents came here, pretty much the first to immigrate here, from India 46 years ago.

My father came here for graduate school. He cleaned vacuum cleaners, and my mother babysat, and they keep telling me about the story of the car that had a hole in it. You could actually see the ground as you drove, and they didn't have enough milk some months. All of my clothes coming here were from the Pennsylvania Dutch lady across the street and her grandchildren. All those stories. My parents were poor. We were poor, but I always think of myself as middle class.

I have to say probably of all the identities that I carry, class privilege is the hardest one for me to embrace and not feel shameful about. When I saw this question, I thought about when I come into the room, into the classroom, I tell my students, "I'm able to stand here in front of you because of so many ways that I have experienced privilege." I think for me it's about that, like you said, I think there's something about class privilege that it affords you certain access.

For my family, it's about education. Educational privilege. To get a master's degree and to get a Ph.D. is seen as, "Well, of course you're going to do that," there's almost a belief that you will have access. You don't have to be white to go through this. When I saw this question, I said, "Well, how can I teach about poverty when I'm middle class and when I don't really know what that feels like?"

Then that led me to try to think about what's the struggle behind this question as a faculty member? I guess for me maybe it's about not feeling legitimate to teach about something that I haven't experienced. I think that's number one. Second, it's about guilt about being middle class. Especially when I hear about the experiences of my students, I'm like, "Oh, my gosh." That puts any of my struggles way down.

May be there is the hierarchy of oppression. There's also the hierarchy of suffering. What's suffering? Maybe I'm feeling uncomfortable that I can't relate to my students on certain levels. An interesting situation came up in class the other day in my undergraduate elective. We were talking about school systems and about inequities within school systems, and then I noticed myself saying things about impoverished communities and schools and the allocation of resources, and then one of my students in the room, he challenged me.

He said, "You know, professor," he basically said that it's not just one story about these schools. There are people who are doing a lot with what they have. I think he made me realize that I was being patronizing in a way. I felt I was being patronizing. In an effort to try and connect with my students around the lack of educational privilege, there was almost a romanticizing of that, and I acknowledged that to the student. I said, "Thank you for saying that" because I was trying to portray schools in impoverished communities that I had no clue whatsoever about because I grew up in a pretty privileged area when it comes to schools.

I guess the question that comes up for me is similar to what Steve said. Do we have to experience something in order to teach about it? I think there's plenty of things that I haven't experienced that I teach about, and I think that one can be fully capable and effective teaching about something that one has not experienced. In fact, if I may have experienced something, I might actually be less effective in ways because I identify with it too much, and then there's another side to this.

I guess maybe it comes down to being able to empathize on a feeling level with experience. You have experiences, and then what are the feelings that come up in those experiences and can I connect with a person around those feelings? I connect to many pieces of what both of you said.

Linda: I'm trying to organize my thoughts because they're going in a lot of directions here. I want to agree with the point that we don't have to have had a particular lived experience to be qualified to teach about it. We're facilitating a process in which we're all exploring that. What do we know from research? We add to that, what do we know from people's lived experiences? In my Introduction to Social Work course, I have done an activity where I ask students to take the federal poverty limit and to try to incorporate their own costs of living into the federal poverty limits just to see how far they could stretch it. How far could you take it?

That has ended up being a pretty eye-opening

experience in terms of what those numbers really mean. Then we're able to have a conversation about how artificial those parameters are and yet how powerful they are in determining what people have access to, which then leads us into this very powerful conversation around policy, around the arbitrary nature of how these things are calculated. What I like about that approach is I just want everyone to try to transport themselves into a situation in which you have less than what you need to function adequately for you, whatever that is.

I feel like if I get them to really think about that, and feel whatever comes up with that, that it's critically important to recognize, therefore, that there are structural forces. Those would probably be my two objectives. Really get it that there are structural forces, and it's not about good or bad people making it. Then really get that "feel," feel some of what it is to not have what you need. I'm thinking about my relationship to poverty.

> *What Is Your Relationship to Poverty?*

Depending on how you calculate it, I'm a second- or a third-generation Puerto Rican. My grandparents came to New York from Puerto Rico as teenagers. My mom was born here. I was born here. They were definitely poor. My grandparents had seven kids. My mother grew up with seven siblings, not enough of anything. Only my grandfather worked as a longshoreman, and my grandmother stayed home and took care of the kids. We had sou-sous. We call them a "sociedad" in Spanish.

I'm very familiar with that, very familiar with the dream of "hitting the numbers," and how important they were, and all the hope that went into the numbers. This belief that at any point your fortunes could change if you were so fortunate to hit the number. Even hitting the number in a small way meant, "We're eating good tonight." I saw that. I was cognizant of the fact that all of my relatives pretty much were poor.

I was cognizant of that, but I didn't think we were poor, but we were. All of my life I qualified for all the stuff, and full financial aid, and free breakfast, and whatever. We qualified for all that, but I didn't think we were poor because what I associated with poverty was based on what I saw with my relatives. Most of my relatives had a lot of kids. It was me and my brother, so I assumed somehow that we must not be as poor because there weren't as many people competing for things.

My mother worked as well as my father. That wasn't the reality in many of my family's situations. My mom was fastidious with the house. Her claim to fame was, "I have two small kids, and you would never know. You could eat off my floors." She was so neurotic about that, and in my other family members' homes, it was more chaotic, more messy. All of those things made me think, "Oh, we must not be poor," because it seems different. I think I really understood that we were poor later, but as a kid I didn't know. I think I was conflating ideas of poverty with a tidy home as a kid.

Like I said, there are a lot of layers here. For example, fast-forward many years ago when I am leading Inwood House, and I feel very compelled that I have to do something around financial literacy for our young women because I realize that there's certain knowledge that gets passed down in some families that I didn't get. Even when I transcended whatever the poverty limits are and was making a good income, in my mind, my identity was still that I was poor, and because I was still poor in my mind, it didn't matter what my paycheck said. It didn't matter what my tax returns said. There were certain things I had to do. I had to buy shoes at Payless. There's a notion that this is how we do it, how we manage. Don't buy anything that isn't on sale, stretch your dollars. It was such a strong part of my identity that there was a real gap between what I had and what I thought I had access to. I have a dear friend, a white woman, who would tease me saying, "Drag your ass to the middle class." One time, while working at Inwood House as the executive director, I bought myself a coat on sale at Kohl's for $37.

I was so proud of my bargain; I thought it was fabulous, and my mother, who never earned what I earn, said to me, "Get rid of that piece of shit. You're an executive director. For crying out loud, buy yourself a decent coat." I was hurt, and I was offended because I thought the coat was actually an amazing bargain for $37. I really did. That was what I was proud of. I was so proud of that.

In 2012, after I got my Ph.D., there were these high-end purses that I admired from afar. I would have never, ever bought myself a purse that was $100, $200. It just wasn't going to happen. Then, I bought myself one. Then I went crazy, and I now have many of these high-end bags. I'm in love with them, but that's a new thing. That's been only since 2012. My husband, who also grew up very poor, and I have shared this idea, and we joke, "We're Bryants; we don't pay full price."

It's something we're proud of. It drives him crazy that I buy these bags because it just doesn't go with who we understand ourselves to be. I've almost had to pathologize it because otherwise why else would I do this? I tell myself I can't help myself. I'm not responsible. I can't do that deliberately. I can't be this indulgent because that would make me somebody else. That would make me like some other ladies, wealthy ladies, those who are not like me. Going back to running Inwood House and financial literacy for the girls, I wanted a consultant who really understood these issues to help me with that. This was a criterion for me. The consultant had to know what it was like to have been poor. I didn't want a "suit" from a big bank to come and say, "We're going to show you," because I really believe that poverty, in addition to being an economic state, is a psychological state. It's a psychology. We have to understand that as well as the economics of it, and people deal with that psychology in a lot of different ways.

Some people are incredibly resilient, incredibly resourceful. Other people are like me in that being poor is part of their identity. "No, that's my identity. This is how we do." We have to understand that. Otherwise we may think that the only answer to this is more resources. Then we get upset when we don't think people are taking advantage of the resources well enough or maximizing it because we think that's the answer, and we have to understand that the answer's more complicated than that.

Steve: You said something really interesting that ties to what Kalima and Mohan mentioned, which is that poverty is both an economic reality, and it can have a psychological impact, and that that has to be factored into this. Which is why, as an executive, you made a decision to make sure that anybody who comes in to train young women once or twice is going to understand that and not just do some aggregated analysis that patronizes and doesn't understand who's in the room. What each of you said, though, that was really interesting was each of you gave a psychological measure that a student corrected for you, in your case, Kalima, about self-care, Mohan, in yours, about what was going on inside schools. I think for teachers, that's a really critical moment. First off, I think we have to do what you said, Linda, which is we have to make sure that we both do the aggregated reality of the "oppression data" with the data that reveals oppression and economic inequality on a structural or historic level.

Then when we get to the psychology, we have to look at how varied that can be and be prepared to do what each of you did because two students, each with not a lot of power, took a brave step to say to you, "Well, that's your experience, not mine. That's your privilege, not mine." In your case Mohan, to say that, you're leaving out a whole group of people who did well. Those are moments of truth for people who teach anything where we're going to deal with these issues of oppression, which is, "We're going to get most of it right, and we're going to get some of it wrong." We have to be open to those with less power to hear us and correct us.

Each of you allowed that to happen where you said, "Oh, jeez, I hadn't thought about that. Thank you," as opposed to what I have had students tell me occurs, and I probably did myself very early on, that when students confront you with something you're not comfortable with, you hide in your positionality of the aggregated data to disguise, "Oh, no, but the truth still is how bad it is," or whatever it might be, rather than saying, "There's other truths that I need to know and recognize."

That's why you know you can teach about poverty, or you can teach about oppression, or you can teach about intersectionality, or racism as a white guy. It's when you realize, "you don't know what you don't know" and thank God there are people in the room with less power than me who can help make sure that we get to the right place.

I'm not going to abuse them when they correct me, which is really the moment when a real shift in classrooms can occur, either for good, where people now are open to being a little safer and more expressive about their stories, or suddenly it's just one worldview all over again. As you made clear, Linda, we all are trying to do that, as difficult and wonderful as that is, because it will bring up our own stories, too, but that leads to a different question!

Guiding Principles and Strategies

As teachers or authority figures or experts of any kind, we tend to feel pressure to be knowledgeable about most things. We need not personally have gone through a particular set of experiences to lead a conversation about those experiences. We do need to be humble about what we don't know and open to listening and learning. As an instructor, am I comfortable with not knowing it all and with learning in addition to teaching? Am I concerned that this will compromise my authority as a teacher? What can I do to lead by listening and learning? How can I create an environment where we all listen and learn?

- Principle: It is possible for anyone to teach on issues of poverty and social oppression as long as he/she is comfortable with his or her own background, whether from social advantage or not.
- Strategy: Practice becoming comfortable with elements of your own background so that if issues are raised regarding social class or other issues of social oppression, you do not disregard them but factor them into the work with comfort. One must be comfortable with one's advantages as well as one's suffering, for in that comfort you will present the richness of this material more fully.

CONVERSATION SEVEN

Question: *"Why do parts of your story matter inside this classroom?"*

Background to this conversation:
This question emerged from our previous conversation where we noted that during discussions of poverty and other forms of oppression, students often explore their own backgrounds as a way of understanding the difficult material. In turn, they look to what experiences faculty members have within their own histories that they can share as well. Such questions create tensions within some faculty regarding professional boundaries within the classroom.

Observations and Reflections:
Many social work academics are committed to social justice and to fighting against oppression based on their own experiences. For some, such as faculty of color or openly LGBTQ, the questions are already in the room and may already be open to interpretation—whether correct or incorrect. How far one goes in such discussions without crossing boundaries that erase necessary academic expectations of performance is an on-going point of reflection for everyone.

THE CONVERSATION

Mohan: I appreciate you saying that, Steve, because it felt like an important moment to assess the use of power and authority in the classroom. This issue of power just happened. It's funny. We're working on this book, and these moments are happening, although I guess they happen other times. There are these moments. When I teach practice I tell them, "You know, you need to give yourself the opportunity to be wrong with your clients. When your clients can tell you you're wrong, that's actually a gift for you and for them." I'm wondering whether I practice what I preach. *Are we open to students disagreeing with us in the classroom? If they disagree, is it a threat to our power and authority as teachers?*

Practicing that in the classroom is not so easy. In thinking about this experience I had in the classroom, I've been in the classroom now 25 years, not just as a social work professor. Before, I was a math teacher, but I started teaching 25 years ago. I definitely, over the years, didn't react the same way when a student corrected me. I was much more defensive, which to me had to do with class privilege, a certain something.

I love the word patronizing. What was interesting, another student challenged this student who challenged me and said, "Actually, the schools do suck, and why should we settle for less?" It led into a whole debate between the two students, which is wonderful, but I think for me, thinking about what you just said, Steve, I said, I'm always curious about how do I as the instructor, manage difficult feelings that come up for me, especially something like this that brings up a lot of shame for me. I feel a lot of shame around coming from a privileged family, and by no means is my family wealthy.

I don't know, but I do come from a family where I was shielded from economic hardships. Whatever my parents were going through, they protected me. I never had to worry about food. They didn't make me pay for things when I was younger. Even when I was an adult, they helped me. I'm able to be a professor right now because of the help they have given me over the years financially to go through graduate school.

When I was a high school teacher, I hardly made any money so I needed help. It's only now in my late 40s that I'm beginning to really deal with the shame that has come from economic privilege.

Then I have to look at why is that so shameful for me? There are plenty of people. Look at Donald Trump—he got a million dollars to start his company.

Steve: He's not ashamed.

Mohan: He's not ashamed at all, no.

Linda: He doesn't pay taxes.

Mohan: He doesn't pay taxes. I pay my taxes though. I've got to look at that, though, because there is a tremendous amount of shame that I feel around my educational privilege, my class privilege, my feeling protected by my family to the point where I don't have to worry—not in the sense that I'm going out and buying expensive things.

In fact, I'm like you, Linda, where I will not buy anything that's not on sale. In fact, I've gone in the opposite direction.

I've become now a professor, and, in fact, I'm becoming more cheap. With pride, I said I went to a store and I got the clearance of the clearance. I got two pairs of shoes for $50, although I realized I bought the wrong size on one of them!

There's something going on for me, which is I'm trying to be somebody I'm not when it comes to this. It's only now that I'm actually articulating this because this is probably one of the final frontiers for me as far as self-awareness. I've dealt with a lot of other stuff. This is one that I have stayed clear from because it brings up a tremendous amount of guilt and shame. I was able to be comfortable in my skin when that student confronted me, but that's after many decades of not being comfortable in my skin around this issue.

Kalima: I think that's part of teaching class and poverty, and I think a great resource for this is *Class Matters* by bell hooks. Part of it is that we can't talk about class without talking about static versus dynamic identities.

There are a few things about identity that can shift. My blackness will not shift. My ability can shift. My mental health status can shift, but you wouldn't know that necessarily. My gender can shift, and depending on what shifts and how it intersects with my race, my class will shift, and when it does, my relationship to material things also shifts along with my sense of self as it relates to class.

Poverty as a mental or psychological experience can rob us of so much. This is particularly true if you've grown up with the idea that the meek shall inherit the earth. It almost feels like the people who suffer the most will get to Heaven. As soon as we stop suffering, we're not as virtuous.

Mohan: If you get those nice pair of shoes or those fancy bags.

Kalima: Class can bring up so much. We could talk about it from different spaces, such as its power to distance you from your family. Sometimes we've got to push the class privilege away to stay closer to family.

Folks who have grown up with a little bit more class privilege can talk about poverty in class. It's an intellectual activity. However, for folks who have grown up in the thick of things, the discussion is from a very different, more painful space. I remind students that it is very likely if they have any sort of ambition to climb the professional ladder, one day they will be in a leadership position.

I remind them that their class status is going to change, and their reality is going to shift. What we're learning about poverty is one thing, how you engage poverty as your own person is completely different, so, yes, this is a policy issue, and it is also so intimate and so personal, and teaching must approach it as such. The professor has to be ready to handle all the possible reactions to this conversation. Students are going to grapple in so many different ways, so it's less about what we experience personally than it is about holding the balance of what comes up regarding the topic.

Linda: This is powerful.

Kalima: It's so deep.

Linda: This one is really deep. Wow.

Steve: You had something else you wanted to say.

Linda: I just want to say, what Kalima just said about how your class can shift, as I moved up in these positions, my economic class level shifted, but I thought, "Okay, my paycheck is shifting. I'm not shifting."

I really wrapped myself in my little cape with the P for po' on it. We joke, "We're so po' that we can't even afford the o-r." I embraced that because that was part of my identity that kept me humble. It kept me real, and it kept me connected to the people that I loved. I didn't have to be separate or different from them.

I didn't have to be in an outsider class because I had all these degrees, or because I have this job, or whatever. I was, in many cases ironically, less visibly well-off than them. They had better cars than I did, even though they did not have my income, but I was embracing the putt-putt car. Putt-putt is what we drive. We drive a putt-putt, and we're proud of that.

Steve: You bought your putt-putt where Mohan bought his shoes.

Linda: Exactly. To this day, we don't own a house, never have. I have family members who never made what I've made who have homes. I have mixed feelings about that. Part of me is going, "You're stupid. Hello?" but the other thing I do to apologize for having moved up in class is I help everybody, and therefore it's okay to make more because I use it to help others.

Now that I've gone crazy with the designer handbags, which is my one little indulgence, I always have to justify it saying, "I didn't ever do that until I had my Ph.D. I was already an executive director over five years when I did that." I had to qualify it. I was not always crazy like that with the bags, and, of course, I still also give to everything, to everybody. I help my family all the time instead of focusing on saving for retirement and doing a whole bunch of other things. Therefore, I'm not a "come-mierda" (That's a shit-eater in Spanish, but it means a person who's stuck up and thinks they're superior to others. I'm not that.), so I'm still down.

Steve: This is great conversation because it speaks to that, in some way, we have to be able to demonstrate the word "struggle" as part of our own lives for people who are in far more struggle than we now are. It's tricky, because we can't overdo that where it suggests false martyrdom.

Linda: Yes, we want to identify with the struggle in real ways with the people who are in the struggle. We come from the struggle; we fought like hell to get to a better place, but we don't want to abandon the struggle.

Steve: I think we're going to end up circling back to this after our other questions because of the issues of shame and guilt and whatever the impasses are that cause us to get stuck with any of these questions. I know for myself that, obviously, I've had the least areas of struggle compared to anyone here or certainly compared to most of my students. What I had to get to was that I have to use my privilege in order to fight oppression rather than be embarrassed about my privilege. As long as I feel embarrassment, I can't be who I am, and I'm no value to anybody. We'll keep going on this one because it's amazing how deep this can be.

Mohan: I just want to say something, though, about your saying that you have the least oppression or struggle. I don't know though. From what you've said about your childhood earlier, I think there's a lot of things.

Steve: Well, I haven't been oppressed, socially oppressed.

Mohan: Socially.

Steve: The age thing may start to impact it, but psychologically being repressed and being personally violated, there's no question that that happened, but it was individualized, familial. It wasn't social oppression. It was individual pathology applied to me. I ended up being bent and being harmed, but it wasn't for social factors. We can trace it back to my father, but another time because it won't fit in the transcript. Okay, let's do the next one. This was deep.

Linda: That was a good one.

Guiding Principles and Strategies

In our current social, political, and economic climate where there is seemingly a high premium on political correctness, legitimacy, and credibility, teaching and talking about race, racism, and other forms of oppression can be an emotionally exhausting task. It leaves many questioning their right or legitimacy to handle such charged content, especially if the professor does not have direct experience where one's identity is questioned regarding, issues such as race or sexuality.

- Principle: Direct experience is not a prerequisite for teaching a topic. The truth is that we all have experience with the content; however, it is varied. There is value in creating space for multiple perspectives that is both objective and subjective in nature.
- Strategy: Professors should acknowledge the multiplicity and complexity of experiences inherent in the room, including within their own histories. Emotionally charged subjects such as poverty and race or sexuality and discrimination can and should be discussed from both a policy perspective and personal narrative. Professors should relieve themselves of the expectation of being all-knowing and instead, create a space of emerging pedagogy.
- Principle: As faculty, we are not blank slates. We have histories of advantage, disadvantage, privilege, oppression. We are not one story. Similarly, our students are not one story. For various reasons, we subjugate some of our stories, our stories become subjugated by others. Our challenge is to compassionately hold all of our stories in the classroom.
- Strategy: Make certain that there is a balance between the objective realities of poverty, exploitation, and oppression, and the variety of resilient ways people living under such conditions have responded. When appropriate, fit in elements of your own struggle and growth related to the topic from within your own changing identity (whether in terms of positonality, status, age, or other characteristics).
- Principle: There will be people in every classroom who have their own stories of hardship and resilience that through your discussion will express a variety of opinions about the same sets of circumstances—if they are expected to share such experience, the teacher needs to expect the same degree of openness.

- Strategy: Be prepared to hold multiple narratives on social and economic issues throughout the class, using the ground rules discussed earlier as a guide to fostering respect and support for different experiences without disregarding the larger social and economic data at play.

CONVERSATION EIGHT

Question: *What does a white, straight, Protestant male like you have to say to a lesbian woman of color from an economically oppressed background like me?*

Background to this conversation:

As became apparent to the four of us over the course of our meeting together, each conversation became more expansive both personally and pedagogically. Nothing made this clearer than this opening question, offered up by a working class, Dominican lesbian a number of years ago. This question led to discussions about authority in the classroom, who is teaching and who is learning, and issues of fairness when grading students who come from schools that did not prepare them well academically.

Observations and Reflections:

- *Even among social justice advocates, "power" is often imagined as a zero-sum game based on if you gain some, I lose some of mine. Indeed, based on this false equation, the misuse of power in all its forms seems to be at the heart of all forms of oppression. While we are committed to ending broader societal forms of abusive power, how willing are we to truly share authority inside our own classrooms and reframe the meanings and negotiations of power?*

- *Students have many reasons to be trustful and/or distrustful of us as instructors from the moment we walk in the room. We need to remember that this has to do with their histories living within a racialized, heteronormative world, which shapes how they see themselves showing up in the classroom. This manifests in feelings of safety and/or unsafety and their willingness and comfort to speak. How do we create spaces with students where their voices are allowed to emerge over time?*

> Heteronormativity is *"a vast matrix of cultural beliefs, rules, rewards, privileges, and sanctions that impel people to reproduce heterosexuality and to marginalize those who do not" (Oswald, Blume, & Marks, 2005, p. 144).*

THE CONVERSATION

Steve: The next question is, uh-oh, *What does a white, straight, Protestant male like you have to say to a lesbian woman of color from an economically oppressed background like me?* I put that one in because I'll never forget that moment. It was my first class of the term, a class in community organizing. This was at a moment in time where, for good reasons, people were testing whether or not white faculty or any faculty were for real about anti-oppression stuff. This particular woman, with whom I later developed a really good relationship, literally, in the very first class of the term, threw that question at me as a way to see whether or not I was for real about being genuinely open to people, where power differentials in all its forms were there.

She clearly was somebody who wanted to see whether or not I had lived my life as opposed to just spoken it around issues of race and all the different kinds of intersectionality. This challenge was a powerful one and I remember my response, "Wow, I guess you have thrown a whole bunch of people off with that one before, right?" She laughed. I said, "And the truth is that my belief is that I will be able to learn from you exactly about the things that you're talking about, while at the same time, hopefully, being able to demonstrate that I have something to offer, that we will do this together."

I could not have done that in the first five years or maybe even the first ten years of my teaching and committing to living in an anti-racist world. It took me many years to be able to develop the capacity to understand that people need to show up in a lot of different ways very openly, and that people often have reason to be distrustful of me without it being about me at all. It's about what their history has been.

To know that and to experience it, and to know that people are going to show up antagonistic towards me, or any of us, and depending on the situation, it's often not about me, myself, and I, it's about where people have lived. As she revealed, as a woman of color who was open about her gayness at a time when that was still something to be at risk, she was a very strong and assertive woman who did not back off. On the other hand, she was never somebody who said, "I'm not sure but … I don't know if I can say this but … " which a lot of women, due to early socialization, often do in the classroom.

She said, "I'm completely sure." What she wanted to do was, she wanted to be respected, and she also wanted to be challenged. That experience was one reason I put that question in here, that there are going to be people who, for all of us, not necessarily out of racial stuff—it'll be different, of course, for each of you—radically challenge us over a different question, maybe with a different type of interpretation.

For white faculty, and especially for white, straight faculty, and especially for white, straight, male faculty, we have to learn that people have a reason to be distrustful of us, unrelated to us. Instead of trying to deny it or prove to ourselves or demonstrate how wonderful we are, we have to start from a position of respect that people have a reason to distrust us. As I'm saying, unrelated to me, and out of that respect, we can create a relationship.

It's the kind of thing where this question is an extreme example of what many white faculty have often said, which is they'll say, "I have very good students who are people of color, and they write good papers, but they never talk. They don't speak enough." What I say to them is, "They probably have reason not to speak, given lots of issues. It may be temperament. There may be people who are shy. There are such people in every racial group, very shy people."

I go on, "There may be historical reasons related to their own story, their own experience, that to be assertive or to say too much too easily, has gotten them in not only deep trouble but has marginalized them and put them at risk." We have to create situations to demonstrate that, that understanding can be worked with over time. It can't be simply be our good intent by saying, "Please feel free to speak," and then becoming upset when they don't.

We have to create situations that allow for their voices to slowly appear in the room—small group, large group. We have to invite people to give a small part of themselves rather than a large part of themselves. We have to demonstrate our vulnerability and our incompletion, as Freire says, in order for people to feel that they can be the opposite that they could be complete, that they can demonstrate that they know a lot.

There's a lot that those of us with enormous privilege have to recognize, that there are reasons unrelated to who we are that may cause people to show up in ways that are initially unsettling to us but, in fact, have to be respected.

Mohan: The first word that came to mind when you started talking, Steve, and I was thinking about this question, was about legitimacy, being legitimate, having legitimacy as the professor or as the teacher. The other thing I'm thinking about is about empathy. I guess I'm struggling with the question.

I go back to the role I play in the classroom and how I think of the role of teacher, like we were talking about yesterday, about wanting to help create a certain learning experience. That helps me with something like this, to say, "Okay, well, I can be open to any of my students' experiences." At least, I would hope I do that. I think it comes up around class, class privilege.

Who am I to be talking about certain kinds of things, especially, where I teach right now where it's a big deal that they're sitting in that classroom right now, whether it's undergraduate or graduate? They did not have the smooth road I had as far as education is concerned to be able to not have to worry about whether I can concentrate or not have to worry about bills, to have a safety net under me, to be able to go straight into college right away, and then work, and then go back to graduate school, and then constantly have the support of my family to be able to get these degrees, and then stand in front of these students.

I think it goes back to really owning that privilege that I have, which I would say, I, in some ways, really don't do. It doesn't really play out for me in terms of race because I think it helps me to be a brown person teaching the students I teach. Right away I've gained some legitimacy being a person of color, but, of course, I don't know what it's like to be white, so I don't know what that would feel like.

Definitely, I feel a sense of, "Okay, I'm glad that they are seeing a person of color teaching them." Then in the class I'm teaching right now, particularly as a gay person of color. The other thing I would say is that I'm conscious of wanting students to feel like they're teachers. I often say in the beginning of the semester, "We are all students, and we are all teachers, and I have power that you don't have." I never try to say, "This is all equal. We're all equal." I'm like, "No. Let's be real here. I have power, and there's a power differential here, and I'm conscious of that. At the same time, I want us to all feel I am not the only teacher in here, that we're all teachers." One way that I do that in my classes is I have the students do these "class facilitations." I'm doing it in one of the classes I teach right now where they get a chance to choose the unit, and then in a small group they have to teach about 30 or 45 minutes of the class. This is in an undergraduate class where it's much longer, so I'm able to do that.

The idea is not so much you're going to present; the idea is that you're actually going to teach. It's based on the readings, and you have to create a handout that you send to me two days before the presentation, and then you can feel free to do the teaching presentation as you wish. The only thing I don't want is, I don't want you to come in with a PowerPoint, but you can come in with ideas for experiential exercises, videos, and, of course, the students find the best videos that I would never in a million years find, the best stuff.

Linda: Collect them.

Mohan: Oh, yeah, I have them. Then they create these amazing handouts. They take it so seriously. When sometimes I hear colleagues question whether students will take doing a presentation like this seriously, I will say they take it super seriously, even more than I would want them to.

Steve: I think that's also because they know you're serious about really meaning it, that you want them to teach as opposed to, this is an assignment I have to get through. I'm making them do it. It could be whatever the heck they want it to be.

Mohan: Yeah, I'm very serious.

Steve: In my experience, if students know that your comment about their value is just a throwaway, they'll throw it away, but if they're perceived as being valued, which is the embedded thing in that question, "Do I have value with you or not?" if they see their value, then lo and behold, people show up valuing what they have to offer.

Mohan: I do feel very proud of the fact that I do that. I do that very, very well and very genuinely.

Linda: It's not just talk.

Mohan: It's not just talk because I feel it. It's interesting because lately I've been feeling less pressure. I'm walking away from my classes feeling like I actually didn't even teach. And, meanwhile, I know I taught. I think after 25 years of being in the classroom, I actually am finally beginning to feel like I don't have to do this myself. It's like a genuine trusting in the students and what they have to offer, really appreciating each of their styles, how seriously they take it, and then I build on it. I actually build on their presentation.

I can build on what they have to say and then teach what I think needs to be taught. It's wonderful with the undergraduates especially. I don't do it so much with the graduate students. With the undergraduates, it works beautifully. I think it's about how do you genuinely find ways for students to teach, for students to express, not just express their opinion. I want them to teach, actually. I want them to be in that role.

Steve: Raise the bar.

Mohan: The students not only reach that bar, they go, time and time again, well over it, and if you get a really good first one, it sets the bar already very high. They're like, "Oh, my gosh, I have to do that? Okay." Then they do it, and they come up with creative ways. That's how I'm relating to that question right now.

> *In my experience, if students know that stating they have value is just a throwaway, they'll throw it away, but if they're perceived as being valued—which is the embedded thing in that question, "Do I have value with you or not?"—if they see their value, then, lo and behold, people show up valuing what they have to offer.*

Linda: I think that question is a challenge. Clearly the professor's being challenged, and there could even be some aggression in that. My inclination would be to ask, "What do you hope I can teach you? What do you want me to teach you? Because you have a question about what I'm going to be able to teach you, right? What is your hope?" I think it lays the groundwork for a contracting about what's going to happen in the classroom. I'd be really curious about what the hope is of what the instructor would be able to teach them.

It's connected to power, and it's connected to lived experience. Part of what I hear in that question is, "Do you have enough lived experience to talk about some of this?" There's an assumption about who you are as a professor. If you are a white, Protestant male, how can you possibly teach on these subjects? Do you have enough lived experience to do that?

Inherent in that question is a request that your lived experience not be the only one that dominates the room. They want their lived experience to have a place which connects to what you're saying which gives them the space to bring their lived experience in there. Seems to me like the answer is the same or no more than what you bring to this class. We're all bringing a certain lived experience to it. I have a role here, and there's some power inherent in that role. In terms of what I'm going to be able to teach, it's similar or equivalent to what you—each of you—would be able to teach in this.

The other part of the question is, what will I be able to learn as a Protestant, white male? Not just what will I be able to teach, but what will I be able to learn from that?

Steve: Absolutely.

Kalima: I'll tell you, as I said in our earlier conversations, the books that govern my life in this work are *Pedagogy of the Oppressed*, *Teaching to Transgress*, and *The People's History*. For some reason, I love *The People's History*. Paulo talks about this idea of the banking system education, and then in *Teaching to Transgress*, bell hooks talks about the ways in which we need to move away from that. What she was saying was not even to use the language of "teach" at these levels.

When we're in grade school, I could teach you how to do one plus one. At our level in our profession, in my opinion, I'm not even teaching you. I'm just facilitating a process. What I have to say to you is just a process. I'm not in this role nor am I sure I want to be in the role of I have to teach you something. I want to be in a process with you. All I have to say is what my lived experience is, and that is my truth, and I'm willing to be in this with you as you tell me your truth. Playing this role of teach, I just, I don't know. It just makes me cringe.

I'm also cringing because I just read an article that I gave to the interns called, "Releasing Victimhood and Taking Responsibility and Accountability," by bell hooks. She says that folks of color need to stop holding onto this idea of victimhood all the time and needing somebody to validate us because the truth is, we know what needs to be said, and we mustn't care what others have to say about it.

How do we have those types of conversations, or how do we move folks of color into those types of spaces of not needing for folks in power to have the answer, not needing for folks in power to validate me in the classroom, Not needing that? How do we move them to knowing that they stand alone, and they stand enough? That is enough.

Linda: Interesting.

Kalima: I know I had all these visceral reactions to this idea of teaching but also visceral reactions to the need to be validated. I know the people don't mean to be this way; we need to be validated. I've been privileged to be able to sit in my room and in my house and read all these books and have access to brilliant minds all the time. My perspective may be a little bit jaded in that sense. All I have to say is my truth. I'm looking forward to hearing what you have to say, and I hope that you'll be open to hearing what I have to say.

Steve: It's funny. Each question we think is going to be a short one, but it never is. Each question gets to other issues. Like what you just said, Kalima, about what bell hooks wrote, "People have to get past the need to be validated for who they are" and so on. That's true, and I have so much experience with people who've been so rarely validated in any part of their lives. At work, the primary reason people leave jobs in human services is not salary. It's a lack of respect. A lack of respect comes from a lack of validation that you have anything to offer, that your brain actually has things to offer.

On the one hand, I think both hooks and you are completely right. People need to stand on their own authority and their own power without the need of another, *and* I think people need to go through a set of experiences to be able to transcend that, to be able to stand like that. Mohan, you said it took you years to be able to trust that what you were doing in the classroom didn't require you to formally teach in order for learning to take place. That took a while. It's funny. I was sitting here thinking, "Where did I start from?"

I started by regurgitating my four-year graduate experience into two-hour lectures where I'd have shell-shocked students looking at me, like, "What?" I desperately believed that the level of content, the content would save me. Right? To now, where students in my practice classes get upset because sometimes I barely mention readings. I'll mention them as an aside, but it's more about what we're doing together. That's because within that teaching/learning experience, I teach in classes where my own book's being used in part. I therefore have a particular reputation, so people come in with certain perceived notions about who I am.

As I've said before, I'm very conscious in my relationship with students to not overplay my formal learning because if I speak too much in an intellectual way and give too many quotations from authors, the power differential between us never stops, and I've got to break that. On the other hand, some students can't understand why I'm not more didactic. They get upset, and they say, "You never talk about the readings. Why do I even have to read?" I have to struggle with coming back to showing some content without imposing the content, and that's hard.

Mohan: That's actually what was coming up for me when you were talking about your struggle around what does it mean to teach, this notion of teaching. Then you, Steve, brought up content, right, this notion of content. While I do want to facilitate a process where their lived experience can be the educator, at the same time, I want to know that I do actually have knowledge that they don't have that I have gained through formal education, that I've gained through a knowledge of theory. I have a knowledge of research. I have a knowledge of these formal ways of knowing that I feel a responsibility to bring into the classroom so that they can then view their own experiences or their experiences with their clients or the world through those lenses. That's why I always tell them these theories are lenses. They're just glasses we put on, and they're not truths.

We interpret them, and then we use them. There are times in classes where I'm very didactic, especially when it comes to teaching theory. Like when I teach practice class, and I'm teaching theories, I realize I need to teach them cognitive theory or I need to teach them object relations.

I think for me there is a role of teaching because I don't know if certain things will organically evolve unless I actually use the knowledge that I've gained through my formal education.

Kalima: It's so interesting because when you started to talk about content, I started to think about what are all the classes that I teach? What are classes that are primarily facilitation versus content-based? Then I was like, well, no, each of your classes is content-based. What is your experience with this? Now that you're talking about it, I need to teach them CBT (cognitive behavioral theory) and object relations.

The way in which I teach it, you feel like you are teaching it, and I feel like I'm facilitating their connections with labels and terms. A quick example is talking about how did poor communities become poor communities, and I talked about the great migration. They didn't formally know about the great migration, but their parents were part of the great migration, or they have friends who were part of the great migration, or they have friends who will say, "I'm going down South," and nobody understood. "What does this term mean, 'I'm going down south'?" Because your family migrated north.

What I did was simply introduce this concept that connected to their real, lived experience where they could all be like, "That's what the hell that meant?" because they've already lived it. When I say CBT, and I'm like, "Have you ever been in this moment where you think this, and you begin to feel that, and shit goes downhill from there?"

Steve: Definitely.

Kalima: We have a great conversation about it, and all I did was put the term CBT on it.

Steve: Then you're bringing the theory to life.

Kalima: I bring the theory to life. I don't ever see it is as me teaching, I just see it as me uncovering. I wonder what my relationship with teaching is, like the term "teaching," or the position of power of a teacher because I'm so like, "No. You already have the knowledge." This is the reason why I feel like this, because I'm coming out of *Pedagogy of the Oppressed*, and I'm coming out of Augusto Boal who says, "The folks already have the knowledge. We just have to create the spaces of which that comes out." I think I really do have to sit with this term.

Steve: The authority?

Kalima: Authority of a teacher and …

Steve: What we were talking about earlier.

Kalima: … own that, and see what's happening.

Steve: You just took the question out of my head. I was just going to ask you, What would it mean for you to then own that authority, that authority of teaching? I guess we interpret teaching in different ways. The way you just talked about teaching CBT is how I teach it.

I use myself, and people come up with personal examples because otherwise the theory is just dead. It's just sitting there, but it's just an interesting thing. I think we have different relationships to what that means.

Linda: I think there's content and process, and I think the way we approach the process is that the process itself is part of the content because when we are facilitating and when you carry out your teaching in that way, that is part of what you're teaching. It isn't separate from the material.

Kalima: Right.

Linda: It's not just a delivery system for the material. It is content, teaching, helping people to question, to bring out their lived experience. That is …

Steve: Content. That is content.

Linda: Content, even though you could say it's process, it's really content.

Kalima: Right.

Linda: It seems to me from our conversation that we have very similar ideas about what teaching is and that there isn't this demarcation between process and content. What we may have different thoughts about is how we manage the power of the position of the teacher. That, I think, we need to explore a little bit, especially for us as people in the field of social work, where we're constantly grappling with issues of power and how that plays out in society.

How do we feel about the power inherent in the role of the teacher, the grades that we're going to issue, the assessment of the work that students turn in? How do we feel about that?

Mohan: It circles back to the original question, which is around, "Who are you in your identities to be teaching me in my identities?" I think maybe the way we relate to this power is all intersected with our other identities. It's like gender, race, ethnicity, class status, educational privilege, all these things that we have, how we all got to the point we're at. I often think about that. How do we get to this point to be able to stand there in front of these students?

Steve: I agree. I think that's a wonderful issue to look at, Linda, that you just mentioned. I know and I think about the content in different courses. In the practice classes, the process is much of the content itself so that it lends itself to more facilitation. Then when I teach to my political economy class, I'm going to speak about global capitalism and the shifts from 19th Century industrial capital to global finance capital in the 21st Century.

That stuff is almost like statistics to people where they get terrified because the language and concepts are so difficult. They can't even link them yet. Eventually, I hope, they'll link them. There's no way I can initiate that course and not spend a lot of time on certain content. What I had to learn to do, though, is when people taught me political economy, they taught it abstractly, and so what I had to learn to do was to tell stories (see Side Box 7), first, from the type of experience that people had in their lives, from which I could then do the theory, as opposed to dominate the theory and intimidate the crap out of people.

I learned to do—I don't know if this happened, Mohan, in our class—but I learned to do the political economy of muffins, where I explained the history of muffins, which I won't go through in detail because it's too long, but it is about social and economic relations. At one time, muffins were just what you had at home made by women, a gendered kind of thing, produced little, and there were only two kinds, bran or corn. Now, we eat big muffins all by ourselves, industrialized by whoever makes them. We don't know the producers, but there are so many muffins now!

Mohan: Like blueberry.

Steve: Women are out of the home, but now we could get a cappuccino muffin. It all speaks to changes in the mode of production, in relations of capital, blah, blah, blah. I had to learn to respect that students would be struggling with this and to locate my theory in their stories first as a way to make them not just be grounded but to give them enough security to struggle through the other really difficult stuff about global capitalism, which is foreign to most social work students.

That all speaks to showing respect for students, which is what everybody's talking about here. That they're going to have something to offer me and I have to work with them, as opposed to, "I'm the great teacher here and will now dominate you by showing you how unbelievably smart I am about political economy." When that happens, they all sit there, and the best we can get out of this is false deference.

Mohan: I remember your class. I remember that I was in that class, 16 years ago. I remember that was a very content-heavy class, probably one of the most content-heavy, if we want to define content as theory and concepts and all these, but it didn't feel like that. If I think back on that class, I remember your lectures, and you had a lot of lectures, but the lectures were needed.

There was no way I was going to understand that stuff by just reading it. There was just no way I would have understood it just through my own experience. I needed the way you explained it, which was in a didactic way, but I don't remember that class being like, "Oh, that was a lecture." It was actually very process-driven.

Steve: I guess when difficult content is presented in ways that respect the student's ability to stretch and learn, and it's not just a chance for the professor to show off how much he/she knows, the sky's the limit. We all get that tasty muffin, only we made it together!

Part of the way to demonstrate that "those without power are as worthy as those with power" in teaching is to sprinkle examples of excellence and smarts and leadership from a variety of people from many walks of life. A powerful exercise to use with people is to ask them to "identify your most significant mentor or teacher, and why he or she still matters to you." Their answers rarely are from formally powerful people and instead are teachers, supervisors, or a relative who had integrity, intelligence, and compassion while keeping high standards. Examples include:

- An uneducated grandmother who taught herself to read and inspired her grandson to stay with difficult tasks.
- A high school English teacher who had been a football player in college and teared up reading poetry.

Guiding Principles and Strategies

Educators as well as social work supervisors see giving their students challenges as an important part of their learning and growth. Of course, seeing the challenge come back at you from someone perceived as having less authority is another matter. Recognizing that such challenges are part of our own development is indeed one of the greatest challenges we will confront in our work, and can and will take demanding effort.

- Principle: When a student makes a substantive challenge to our work, it is our responsibility to interrogate ourselves first as to whether or not such a challenge is sincere so that our response demonstrates respect to the student without foregoing one's own contribution.
- Strategy: Allow yourself time to sit with the question or comment before responding by saying you will honestly consider such a comment and—not but—you need time to reflect on it. It is thus critical that such reflection leads to a response either later during that session or in the next class.
- Principle: Some challenges are less about you yourself and the content you offer than a student's previous experience and accumulated stories that led to their comment.
- Strategy: Acknowledge the comment, followed by a respectful use of "AND."

CONVERSATION NINE

Question: *"I DISAGREE WITH ..." How do we help students distinguish microaggressions from simple disagreement in the classroom?*

Background to this conversation:
Many faculty report being flummoxed on how to handle disagreement in the classroom over social issues out of fear that either the discussion will become uncontrollable or that people will feel hurt in ways the faculty cannot resolve.

Observations and Reflections:
Many of us in the field are averse to conflict itself, whether in the classroom or elsewhere. Arguing over ideas, therefore, can be a challenge. How can we help students make these necessary distinctions if we ourselves are struggling with conflict itself?

THE CONVERSATION

Mohan: Okay. This is a classroom question. *"How do we help students distinguish microaggressions from simple disagreement in the classroom?"*

Steve: Since I put that question here because many faculty have approached me on this issue, I'll start. Over the years, what I've learned to do is that I'm prepared for this to happen. I'm prepared both for students who have been oppressed to hear things that cause them to not be able to make that distinction between simple disagreement and a microaggression, and I'm prepared for a lot of white, privileged students to probably say things that they don't know are offensive.

What I've learned to do is to start with a little bit of my own struggle to learn. At some point, relatively early in the past, I model my own ignorance from the past because I grew up in a—laughingly, but it's no joke—I grew up in a town where the minority were white Catholics. I'll say that I didn't know what I didn't know. I didn't know that what was safe for me by being an assertive person in the classroom was perceived as a strength where it would be used against a woman or a person of color, that somebody can be perceived as being aggressive, where for me, I'm just being perceived as dynamic.

I used that kind of example early as sort of a preemptive item so that when something later happens, it's understood, where I've had white students say, "I'm scared by what you just said," saying it to, say, a young woman of color who had been excited about something but not hostile, not aggressive toward anyone, just excited about an issue or topic. I'll pause, and I'll say, "It's interesting because I want you to go back to what I talked about in my own struggle, how it's so easy to misperceive some other person being 'excited' as opposed to being 'aggressive.'" I ask them to reflect on their fear because that fear is often associated in ways that cause people unlike you and me—white people—to get arrested, to be vilified, to be perceived as somebody dangerous.

Then, when issues come up where there'll be disagreement, and a white student often will say, "Well, I disagree about that because you think our society has always been unfair, but in my experience … " Then people of color, young people of color, will take offense that this student is putting them down. My work, at that point, is to say, "Isn't it interesting? We've got to go back to those ground rules, right? Can we distinguish 'disagreement about the idea' as opposed to 'about the person' where somebody is perceiving you as 'less than'? Everyone here has to work off others' ideas, not challenge their humanity." These are moments that happen maybe twice a term. Sometimes they only happen once a term, but they're incredibly powerful to work with because if they're not worked with, the class is done for the term.

If that disruption and upset is worked with right then, even though it takes us away from the lesson plan, even though it takes us away from what the content was supposed to be, then deeper learning for students is really happening. It took me many years to get comfortable with that disruption. I've been teaching a lot of years. It took me a long time to become comfortable with the fact that this was a moment of great importance, that even though I was sidetracked, the content of the hour or the day was technically over, that shift was going to be necessary.

The message that I would want other faculty to have on this is that when these moments occur, they're going to be difficult, and the learning is deeper than the learning about the curriculum content of the day. Just remember though, for me, I get all the advantage of doing this as the older white guy—and previously as the younger white guy or the middle-aged white guy—so I have a lot of capacity to be able to do this in ways that are riskier for everyone else in this conversation. I think with each of us in this room, it's going to be a very different experience given who each of us is.

Kalima: I'm reflecting on why this question is so difficult for me. Part of the reason why I feel it's so difficult is because how do we say to folks of color that that is not a microaggression? Right? How do we say that? The truth is, their perceptions are all dependent on what phase they are in of racial identity development. One of the things I've been reflecting on with students is when they're first awakening and getting the language and reading all the articles in the books, everything feels like a micro-aggression, right? That's just part of the process. It's part of them becoming very, very clear about who they are in the world and putting labels on the actions that they've always endured or to the things that they've always experienced. Now they have labels to put on it.

How do I help them to not see it as a microaggression? I don't know if I've ever done that. I can't say because I'm way too afraid to add to the history of further invalidation of what they have experienced. That's what I'm struggling with. What could be a disagreement that doesn't feel like a microaggression in a situation where there's an inherent power differential? I don't know of one. Maybe if somebody gave me an example of a situation that is a disagreement but not a microaggression that may be helpful to me, but I don't know of any in this context.

Mohan: I'm struggling with the question, too, in terms of relating to it. It makes me think, how do I handle disagreements in the classroom? Part of it is where I teach. I teach in an institution where there are very few white students, not to say there's not other forms of diversity, but the racial makeup of where I teach makes a difference in how these kinds of conversations happen.

There's certainly disagreements that happen. I'm kind of the opposite of you, Kalima, where you have a hard time not seeing it as a microaggression, then I might be on the opposite end.

Kalima: Of seeing it as a microaggression?

Mohan: Yes, I have a tendency to avoid seeing it as a microaggression. Just thinking about it out loud right now, part of that is I'm realizing, through this whole process as we're talking about all these questions around race, how much I de-racialize myself in this country.

Linda: Could you say more about de-racialize?

Mohan: Well, to deny that I have experienced racism. I think for most of my life, I tried to pretend I was not brown. It's only as I became older that I started to feel good that I'm brown. I think I mentioned it in another question that part of that is the history of my family, coming here as Indian immigrants to a very white area in Pennsylvania. It was not safe to be open, you know like we're going to be Indian, and we're going to be out there. There were microaggressions happening non-stop all the time, in addition to full-out discrimination. I think that what's happened for me is I've swallowed a lot and not let myself see things as actual microaggressions against me, so then I think I bring that into the classroom. I've personally intellectualized a lot of it. Being an academic gives me a nice place to do that again. I'm wondering why it's not resonating for me, this question. All the other questions kind of struck at my heart; this one is bouncing off my heart.

It's kind of like, oh, my gosh, what kind of professor am I? I don't have anything to say about this. It's not that students don't share things in my classes. There's a part of me that's not wanting to see it in that way, as microaggressions. Part of it is maybe fear of conflict, fear of conflict in the room.

You talked about power, so I do bring that up a lot in class about who has the power to name things, who has the power to ask the question of another person. We were talking about it in one of my classes the other day, about invisibility and visibility. We were talking about who has the power to make somebody else invisible or the reverse of that, who has the power to scrutinize somebody else? That kind of stuff I definitely talk about it, but I'm realizing I've experienced so many microaggressions in my life that my coping mechanism through my life has been to rationalize it. That's what I mean by de-racialize, although now with this current climate, I'm wondering when am I going to cross the street, and somebody is going to say, "Get out of here!" or, "What are you doing here?" Then I'm going to flash out my passport, my American passport.

Linda: I told my husband jokingly, that if somebody said something to me like a racial epithet, I would respond by saying first of all, when you call me that, make sure you say, "Dr." first! Get it straight. Then I would clock them, like really just [sound of hitting a fist together]. The last thing they'd remember before going down was that they were decked by Dr. ___ fill in the epithet. *(Everyone laughs.)*

Anyway, you got me thinking because what I was going to say, my thinking about this question is that a microaggression is in the eye of the receiver, right? There is no way to objectively define it. There's not an objective measure of a microaggression. It's subjective to the person who experiences it as a microaggression. The person who delivers it may or may not have had intent or may or may not have had conscious intent in delivering it. Somehow in the ground rules, I would want to establish that everything to some degree is subjective and that our responsibility in the room is if you feel that you've been micro-aggressed, you should say that. I would want people to experience enough power to say, "That didn't sit well with me" and for the other person to be able to say, "Well, that's not what I meant, I meant this," and out of that exchange, hopefully comes some insight and some understanding that whatever your intent was or wasn't, it was received this way. Why was it received that way? What goes into that? Why did you deliver it that way?

If we get to those kinds of dialogues in the classroom, I would feel satisfied that there's a level of authenticity and struggle with trying to unpack that, but I'm wondering, after hearing what you said, if that's just my own way of rationalizing, too? Just wondering if I'm comforting myself with the thought that if we can own it, then that's rather advanced of us. If owning it is a good thing, that may also protect me from maybe feeling the rage I would feel if I didn't give the breathing room, the cover of the intention. If I just allowed myself to feel offended, too, if there's an exchange in my classroom, and someone feels offended, what if maybe I feel offended, too? Instead, I'm going to push that aside and tell myself that my job here is to promote dialogue and—

Mohan: Facilitate.

Linda: Facilitate and whatever, but what I'm not doing is plugging into how I experience that, and I may not also feel like it's my place as the person of color to stand next to the person who feels offended and be the advocate and defender.

Mohan: Right, because you feel like you're playing sides?

Linda: Because I feel like I'm playing sides and mostly because I have to, maybe, protect the feelings I have of not really liking what you said, and maybe not liking you, and I am not allowed to do that, and that leads to another question of how do we facilitate difficult conversations of class content.

Guiding Principles and Strategies

Creating a classroom climate where people are able to simply disagree and not perceive it otherwise takes preparation both with one's handling of conflict itself and in allowing people to experience their world without invalidating it.

- Principle: Holding what may be conflicting truths is not easy, yet it is necessary to be effective.
- Strategy: Besides making certain your ground rules cover how to handle perceived slights as well as disagreement, work on growing comfortable with holding different points of view without shutting down. Work from there to deepen students' insights and approaches to such topics so that you do not neutralize and trivialize the exchange as simply "respecting differences."
- Principle: As people become attuned to dynamics of oppression at both the macro and micro levels, there necessarily will be extreme responses based on their stage of "developmental awareness" that need to be understood as the teacher or facilitator responds to different voices inside the room.
- Strategy: Be conscious of maintaining an even, respectful tone with all participants as you develop the mindful lens of holding multiple truths being expressed by students. Such an approach models ways for students and others to break from binary, "either right or wrong" thinking that otherwise can solidify people's thinking about the various forms of social oppression in our world.

CONVERSATION TEN

Question: Is it possible to be an objective facilitator of class content on socially charged issues?

Background to this conversation:
Because of the intensity of the previous material on handling classroom discussions, the group decided to deepen this by exploring the tensions and opportunities from our own backgrounds as such material is broached inside the classroom.

Observations and Reflections:
This kind of social material obviously connects powerfully to many faculty's own stories. How comfortable are you with integrating such a story into the classroom, without compromising the desired give-and-take you seek as necessary for learning?

THE CONVERSATION

Mohan: Tying this question—*Is it possible to be an objective facilitator of class content on socially charged issues?*—to the last conversation, Linda, do you feel like you have to be objective with the content itself, even as students become upset?

Linda: Right. I'm just questioning whether this commitment, which I just felt so comfortable with, of being objective, is really a way of trying to make this much more civilized than it really is and not get in the muck and mire of ugliness, the real ugliness that can be there.

Mohan: I think, Linda, from what you're saying, two things come to mind. One is, all professors are racialized beings. It's very interesting because all of us have these different responses to this. I think it came up in another question about this whole notion of objectivity and us being these, you know, our role as the professor. Facilitating and …

Linda: Above the fray in some ways.

Mohan: … in a way and part of that is I think necessary because we do play a role. I play a role in that room, and I am not one of my students. I have to be in it and also outside of it, and all of that stuff. At the same time, it's slippery. What I realize is that my own defense when I feel hurt or I feel scared of something is to intellectualize, to reframe. I mean, this whole thing of reframing is actually an exertion of power, right? I can try to diffuse an emotional situation through a reframe, and then the student doesn't have the power to change that because I then have exerted my power to take something that was racially charged or anything charged, and because I'm uncomfortable and then I can hide behind the role—for me, I'm not saying for you—I can hide behind the role of the facilitator as opposed to allowing it to get emotionally messy, which kind of relates, I think, to the next question. That's what's coming up for me. I guess I'm becoming more sensitive to that because I'm realizing in my personal life I'm doing it less and less. I'm less defensive around my emotions and letting myself feel hurt and angry, but when you're in that role as professor it's kind of …

Steve: It's tricky.

Mohan: It's tricky. It's a weird space.

Kalima: It's very tricky.

Mohan: It's not group therapy. You're talking about personal stuff in an academic environment. It's complicated.

Linda: I am questioning whether it is a use or misuse of power though, in that role to try to make this all very objective and very facilitated, or you could just say that you feel this way and acknowledge it, and is that being true to, you know, the real pursuit of justice? Isn't it very powerful and lofty of me to be able to keep this all contained and facilitated, which is part of the role, I get it, but if the same thing happened outside of the classroom, would I think about it the same way? Or would I be quick to jump in and say, why did you just say that? Why did you talk to her that way? Right? I'm just questioning that, like, how true and sincere it is to the ideals that we're about.

Steve: This is great stuff. First off, it's really great that each of us, given our own identities and histories, has a different response to how to deal with this, which speaks to how much the classroom itself is a social construction of how learning takes place or not. That comes across.

As you were saying, Linda, one thing I'm always aware of not only when I'm in an agency but also when I'm in the classroom is I'm always saying, "Are we safe enough here where I can say I disagree with you and you don't say to yourself, 'Is he disagreeing with me because I'm a (fill in the blank)?' Is she saying that to me because I'm a … ?" As long as that unspoken question is in the room, that room is not a place where full problem-solving and full give-and-take is going on, so the learning is being compromised in some way. Something is being compromised in that way, so the struggle to create that open learning environment is compromised. Your point, Linda, though, is if somebody does something that we perceive is offensive, and somebody feels it as a microaggression, is it our responsibility to side with them and say, "Hey this has to happen," or do we learn a different response, like, "Hey, this shit has to stop"? Of course, that's not a nice way to actually say it, but where you openly confront someone with, "Do you see what you did? That is horrible."

Or do we find something else to say to say, like "Could you see how this lands?" There's more complicated but necessary ways. "Do you see how this lands, when I hear your intent, can you hear her response? Can you see that she's been hurt?" As facilitator, be able to go through that in a way that neutralizes some of the antagonism, some of the tension, so that discomfort is still there but not entrenched conflict.

In my experience, if we do take sides, if we either are siding with somebody or making believe conflict between two points of view never happened, then the classroom's done as a learning experience where people will never engage again.

In some ways, I'm working on the greater good of the learning experience, which is different than my political belief related to who's right or wrong. In order to foster a kind of climate that will allow people to be able to genuinely hear it's just a disagreement, or if the language is misused, the aggressor, the micro-aggressor, understands what he/she has done, or that the person who perceives the microaggression, he/she perceives that he/she has to struggle with the discomfort of being disagreed with as opposed to being diminished. God, that's hard.

Kalima: It is, and I'm not sure if we're ever going to live in a world where that is actually possible. I don't think that we will ever live in a world where someone disagrees with us—whether they are within our race or outside our race—where we don't have a second thought, are they disagreeing with me because I'm a woman, because of this because of that, because those are our systemically marginalized identities, and we're socialized to …

Mohan: Be sensitive.

Kalima: Be sensitive to it but also to dismiss what those folks who hold those identities have to say. Conversely, on the other side of that, there are spaces in which folks will agree with me because of my identity. How then does that work out? It works out on both ways. That's one of the things that I wanted to say. The other thing that I wanted to say is, something you said, Linda, because you keep saying how would you handle that, like your process through this.

Linda: Mm-hmm (*affirmative*).

Kalima: I'm saying what's the alternative? Right, what's the alternative in the classroom because we are playing a role in the classroom? I oftentimes will go over to folks, I will be very, very honest and say, "Whoa, I'm part of this class." I set it up that I'm part of this class, that I'm also in a journey with them, learning from them as they are learning from me, and while I know I hold power, I'm also a human in this class and sort of just seeking to be with other humans, and sort of acknowledge that what was said made me slightly uncomfortable, and I'm willing to enter into a journey with them if they are willing to enter it with me, really, owning the power I have in that classroom because I do want to model what is possible in the world.

Going back to the original question of microaggressions versus disagreements, I don't know if they're mutually exclusive. I think you can microaggress, and it can be a disagreement at the same time, and that's okay.

Mohan: In a way, the microaggression can be worked with. It's not a done deal.

Kalima: Right. We don't need to term it as a disagreement for us to be able to work with it or for us to work through it. It can just simply be a microaggression. In some of these classes, folks are just literally brand new to these types of relationships; they have no clue. I'm in a class right now with a girl from Texas, and she says you would be hard-pressed to find a black person in her town, so all these folks that she's dealing with right now, this may be her first encounter with people who do not look like her, who are not from her class background, in these very intimate ways and having these very intimate conversations. Is she going to make a mistake? She sure is, unless she is not going to open her mouth. I don't know. I'm still struggling with the idea of having it be separate.

Mohan: I think you said it really well, that it doesn't have to be … Well, I think it's that the microaggression can be worked with. I think it's important to call things microaggressions because that has a specific meaning, right, as opposed to disagreement, because it has to do with power. Something you said, Steve, was helping me think about this whole thing about role, our roles. It goes back to what you were struggling with based on what I was saying, that our responsibility is to the learning experience. That's the thing. The space that I help co-create with my students creates opportunities for a learning experience.

I think that in relation to when I teach this course on LGBTQ issues. Because you get a range of experiences in that room in terms of people's sexual orientation and gender identity, attitudes tend to be kind of generally open, like you don't usually get a student in there who's saying, "I hate gay people." That's probably not the person who would take that class, but there are the same kind of issues around, "What do I say? How can I say it?" I think what I'm realizing is, how do you do it so that you are teaching in a way that serves justice? What I'm realizing, at least I'm just going to put this out there, is that maybe that's actually not what the goal is because that's an outcome that I cannot control as the teacher. All I can do is help to create a learning experience, and the students create their own outcome.

In a way then, it's not about siding so that we're on the side of justice; it's about how do I create the space for both of those people in the room so that there's a learning experience?

Linda: In part, I agree, and I agree with my original thought which is, my job is to provide an opportunity for them to unpack what did I mean by that, what did I hear, to have that exchange, right? But as a social work professor, not just a professor, right? As a social work professor, I do feel like I have to be mindful about justice, and if a form of injustice is playing out in the classroom, certainly as the teacher I have to turn it into a learning experience, but I also can never not be an advocate for justice.

Mohan: You're not neutral in that. You cannot be neutral.

Linda: That's the next word I wanted to come back to, where you were talking, Steve, you said about not neutralizing the situation, and I think that we have to be very careful not to aim to neutralize too quickly, that we have to really be able to tolerate the discomfort and push for unpacking some of that and not try to make it okay too fast. That's part of the inclination we really have to resist, just like we have to resist the inclination to get in the aggressor's face and say, "Why did you do that? Say you're sorry." We also have to resist the inclination to neutralize it too quickly if it's going to be aligned with what we were talking about in earlier sessions—authenticity—and it's going to be aligned with the point that you cannot do this work, you cannot learn and grow if you try to keep everything on an intellectual-only level.

Mohan: I'm just going to throw this in very briefly. To me, it also connects to the debates about research, about the goals of research, the idea of research having a social justice aim, this whole idea of the paradigms that say that research is about not having that kind of bias. People who critique it say, "You're already imposing a bias on the whole research enterprise by saying it's got this aim for social justice." Then the critical theorist says, "Hello, why are we doing the research?" You know, social work research needs to be ultimately in the service of people, right? I mean, otherwise what's the point of doing this?

It's kind of a philosophical question in a way that plays out in research, about neutralizing research and people who say that's what research needs to be and others who say no.

Kalima: We've got no time, no space for that.

Steve: The other thing that's built into this that I also want to address is what I call the eggshell phenomena. Which is that when people walk on eggshells in academia, rather than confront what they really feel or believe, and instead discussions go back and forth in contortions of not wanting to raise something where they see the microaggression, and then later they're upset with what happened, or somebody else, who perhaps comes from an advantaged background, being so afraid to even state the mildest disagreement or other point of view that they end up falling all over themselves to agree on things that barely matter. Neither individual ends up being able to do this work better a year later—or wanting to work together.

I think for the readers of this guide, this is the kind of thing where this is going to be an area of struggle that everybody's going to have. We're all going to have to take into consideration how difficult this is, yet there's no simple answer. It's really going to be about, are you willing to take this on toward the idea of justice? I know for myself when I'm doing organizing, like I was involved in Occupy Wall Street, people would say stuff, and I'd work real hard to say, (I'm making an "I statement,"), "I think you're really, really wrong because ..." as opposed to what I attempt to do in the classroom, which is, not to repeat myself, try to create that other learning experience, even though there's somebody saying something that I find personally offensive and wrong. I make that distinction because to me the classroom really has to be a laboratory for inquiring, where people first get to grow. If they don't make mistakes, if they cannot grow from their mistakes, if as soon as a mistake happens they shut down, the learning is over.

Linda: I think I want to underscore for our readers, though, that while we're playing a neutral role in the classroom, we're not neutral, that depending on who we are, we will hear something potentially as a microaggression or not, that we're not neutral filters, right? We will have certain reactions to that, which is why I think it's really helpful to think about a question like this beforehand because it's going to happen, and you're going to have some kind of reaction to it, depending on who you are, what you're lived experiences have been, and what that exchange actually ends up looking like.

Kalima: Let me tell you something, I agree, and I want to say Howard Zinn taught me, "There's no standing still on a moving train." There's no such thing as being neutral. Even when something happens in the classroom, I own, I want to practice owning that with the students. I want to practice owning, like that didn't feel right to me.

Mohan: What is owning? For you, what does owning mean?

Kalima: Being very, very honest about what I'm feeling. When a student says out loud, I don't know if I told you all this, but we were talking about suicide, and she says, "Oh, it's this phenomenon where people use suicide by cops. They die by cops." She said it out loud as if it was concrete, and everybody's like, "I've never heard of that, can you explain?" And she's like, "Yeah, you go in front of a cop, and you do something provocative, and they kill you." I said to myself, "Wow, she's tone deaf" because this was during the time when Philando Castile was murdered. He was sitting in a car with his family, professed he had a gun, was following instructions, and was still shot. You cannot make a comment like that in a context like this.

Mohan: Owning for you is, you're acknowledging with yourself, your true feelings. Then what do you do with that in the classroom?

Kalima: I say it. I say, "I'm going to be completely honest, I'm having a reaction to that, and I would love to journey with you, and I want you to help me better understand where you're coming from."

Steve: See, that's powerful, though, because you combined both that you're feeling something that's triggered you, and you're willing to engage with that individual. That engagement over that statement is the hard part.

Kalima: That is the hard part. But you know what else annoys me so much, and I guess because I'm no longer in my fiery stages, is that every time something happens, in order for us to feel like we're doing the work or to be perceived as such, it has to be like we're dragged out, knocked down, yelling and screaming, getting in people's faces, saying, "I'm holding these people accountable, all these racial microaggressions. I'm tired of you white people." I'm like, okay, "Is this the only way this work can look?"

I get it. I get the anger. It is possible that if you map folks using racial identity development, there's a stage of complete anger, and that's their only and/or chosen form of expression, and, the truth is, they get to be there; we all get to be there. I'm going to allow you to be there, but I'm also going to model for you where ten years of organizing around this work is going to get you because you cannot and you will not survive that way. You're just not going to survive. It's going to eat you up, and it's going to eat you alive.

I want to journey with you because I don't understand. Like when men throw around the rape word, and I'm confused by that, you just get to throw it around? I have the reaction, and because I've been with you for twelve weeks or ten weeks, I know you didn't mean to do this, but we definitely do need to journey together on this because I don't understand the use of the rape word.

Mohan: See, you're also modeling, Kalima. You're modeling for me. I'm thinking about Carl Rogers, and he talks about authenticity and really being present, a certain transparency as the instructor. I'll self-disclose or be transparent about something in the classroom, but it's usually not in reaction to, like the way you just said it, what somebody said. It makes me think how as the instructor, I've defined my role in there as the teacher, and then my relationship to them. It's almost like a separation I create.

You're making me realize ... That's why I asked you what do you do with that feeling, and then when you said, Yeah, you actually say I'm having a reaction to what you said, that makes me think, wow, as the professor would I feel comfortable saying that? Like, I'm having a reaction to what a student said, because then it takes me out of that role of being the facilitator. Although, you're still in the facilitator role, so you're doing both, which is kind of an interesting thing.

Kalima: Transparency and authenticity sort of messes around with power, the relationship, the power in the relationship. I was even thinking to myself, what is the difference between Linda and I? Could Linda do this in her classroom? I don't know if you could.

Mohan: Why is that?

Kalima: Because I think that how people perceive me makes it allowable for me to be so vulnerable where I don't know if they would make it allowable for Linda?

Mohan: What is it about how they perceive you?

Kalima: I think they perceive me as closer in age, but I'm not. They perceive me as hip and young, and I have a particular aesthetic and style so they perceive me as cool.

Mohan: So all the things that I'm not? I'm not hip, I'm not young.

Kalima: Right.

Steve: Linda has a very professional suit on today. *(Everyone laughs.)*

Kalima: I'm also not part of the institution, I'm an adjunct. You can take this back to the Trump and Hillary thing. She's thought of as the status quo. You are part of the administration. There are things that I can do. There's a level a vulnerability that I can have that I don't think Linda can. There's a level of transparency sort of like …

Linda: And a level of outsiderness that you can have, right? That allows you to take that risk. As I heard you describe that, I was thinking that approach felt right to me because it's authentic. I am modeling—I haven't lost the ability to facilitate—but I'm also modeling how we have an authentic conversation by taking the risk and putting myself out there. Again, I go back to these—if we're talking about social work—students, I feel an extra responsibility that everything I'm modeling, that there is a parallel process to that, and everything I'm doing is a model for how I think a responsible professional social worker needs to operate, so that actually to me feels like justice also.

Kalima: Mm-hmm *(affirmative)*. Mm-hmm *(affirmative)*.

Linda: By acknowledging that I'm having a reaction to it, I'm not denying who I am, even though I'm in this role as the teacher in the front of the room, and I'm also taking the risk to step out of the power of being the teacher in front of the room to be a human and say I have a reaction to that.

Mohan: All of that can happen at the same time.

Guiding Principles and Strategies

It is as normal as it is inevitable that faculty will be emotionally triggered by student statements, sometimes negatively, sometimes positively. Being aware of this normal reaction, practiced over time, can allow one to not accidentally respond with too much intensity that would undermine classroom norms.

- Principle: There will be great internal effort by any faculty who seeks to sustain these conversations. It will be necessary to distinguish your role as an educator facilitating an attempt at give-and-take in the classroom from your own beliefs without giving up your beliefs or allowing active microaggressions or prejudice to flourish.
- Strategy: Work on your tone and body language so that you are able to speak to both sides of a disagreement without taking sides. At the same time, allow yourself to speak to any discomfort that emerges from a discussion without misusing the power of your position to squelch differing points of view. (Those ground rules are for you, too!)

CONVERSATION ELEVEN

Question: *"I'm HURT!" How do I respond to students' strong emotions to difficult content or reactions to each other and to the content?*

Background to this conversation:
Many faculty have noted that the material in social work, from domestic violence and incest to the deaths of young men of color by police and the shame and violence directed at LGBTQ people from their own families, is necessarily painful and often connects to students' own experiences that spark deep emotionality. The profundity of these connections often electrifies the classroom, leaving faculty in an undeniably tenuous position of aiming to do no harm yet sometimes unclear how to not do so.

Observations and Reflections:
Almost all social work faculty have backgrounds one way or another that have been touched by either social oppression or personal, familial dysfunction and/or loss. Proximity to or direct experience with oppression can serve as a critical source of information to help deal with what comes up in the classroom. Given our own backgrounds, how prepared are we to handle the deep emotional upset that may occur over the course of a semester with our students as we address such difficult content?

THE CONVERSATION

Linda: The question that begins this conversation is: *"I'M HURT!" How do I respond to students' strong emotions to difficult content or reactions to each other and to the content?*

Mohan: Well, that happens a lot actually in my classes. I want students to feel that their deepest emotions are welcome in the classroom, and I really want to use it as an opportunity. It just happened in the class the other week in my LGBTQ elective where the students were doing their presentation, and at one point this one student did a lovely experiential exercise with the students in the class, and I was involved with it. I didn't create it, they created it. It was about coming out and was quite a beautiful exercise. I also know some of my student's history from her journals, so I know that this is very personally relevant for her.

She did it in this very poised, really mature, very beautiful way, and then she got to the point where she posed the question to the class: So why do you think I had you do this? Then some students said something, and then she just broke down in tears. Usually, when students cry in the classroom, their first reaction is, "I'm sorry," and I immediately say, "There's nothing to be sorry about. As social workers we need to cry." I have them explore so what would happen if you actually shed tears with your client? What would that mean? There's this kind of notion that I'm not supposed to cry, and it's almost like the same thing with the professor thing—am I giving up my role? No, you're keeping your role and being vulnerable, so similarly I can be a social worker and cry and be there for the client. I can be both.

She cried, and then she ran out of the room. She needed to. I think in those moments, what I do when a student is so vulnerable is, I really focus on them. I notice what happens to me. I think about Donald Winnicott and what he says about the holding environment, holding that student like a parent would and also holding that space.

In those moments, that's when I really realize my presence is very important. How I respond in that moment is critical, and I always treat it as a gift, you know? Whether it's tears, whether it's anger, whether it's whatever it is, I think those emotions are gifts. I do realize that it's a very tender time in the classroom and how I become really laser focused in those moments in the emotional energy that's happening and really connect with that student who's experiencing those emotions to basically convey it's okay. I think what happens with students is, they kind of get surprised because they think they're not supposed to feel these things in a classroom. Again, it's the social construction of the classroom, that the classroom's not this place where you're supposed to feel strong feelings. I really, really feel strongly about challenging that whole notion and really challenging this kind of artificial division we create between intellect and emotion, rational and irrational, our bodies and our mind, all these splits we've created. It's not like we're studying chemistry, although even there I could be emotional, too. But how could you not be having emotions in the classroom, strong emotions in the classroom, when we're social workers?

I really want them to know. I tell them from the first class, whatever class I'm teaching, especially practice, this is my bias, but I want you all to know that I don't believe in that whole notion of leaving yourself at the door. When you come in here, into this classroom, or when you sit with your client, not only all of you is there, but your entire history is there, every single person who's ever been in your life is there. Your whole family is sitting there with you. I bring in object relations and say everybody who's ever been in your life is all there. You've internalized everybody, so how are you going to leave yourself? What does that actually mean? Leave yourself at the door. Then who's left? There's nobody left to come in.

Linda:	Send a shell in, right?
Mohan:	I tell them this is my opinion; you're going to hear this differently from other professors. I'm letting you know that it doesn't make any sense to me. I'm not surprised that it's hard for students because the classroom has not been constructed as this place for emotions. I don't think so. It's almost like the emotions are a threat.
Linda:	Right.
Mohan:	And I'm like, no, they're not.
Linda:	A threat to order, a threat to all kinds of …
Mohan:	A threat to order, a threat to understanding, to academic knowledge. The student who gave that presentation, she was poised, she was prepared, she knew the material, she read the research, she did this beautiful experiential activity which was a wonderful thing. At a certain point, she felt it so deeply that she … Then the two students who came after her, they all cried, too, so it was like, I love it. I love it when there's strong emotions in the classroom, whatever they are.
Linda:	I agree with your framing it as a gift because I think it is to the entire community, and I've had it happen two times this semester. I felt like it really changed the dynamic; the group became more intimate just because it happened. Same thing, I feel like okay, it's the holding environment, and I want to communicate comfort, like I'm not freaked out that you're crying, so nobody needs to be freaked out, and I think for this profession, again, in particular, we're training professionals who are going to help people manage emotion. So we're going to do that by not managing emotion? You know, like pretending there's an emotion, I don't see it, okay on to the next

thing, right? We have to model it, model the comfort with it. One of the things I struggled with both times where this happened was to resist the thinking that it was all on me to respond. I had to remind myself, this is a community. I'm one member of this community, and I have a designated role in this community, but also let the community jump in, and they did.

Steve: That's great.

Linda: That's what helped build the intimacy.

Steve: There are two other responses besides the one where people cry because something's touched them so much. I experience this, not a lot, but a couple of times a term. One is anger, and the other is fear. The other is the hurt or the struggle that people are going through. Your point, Mohan, in either case to do it with sort of a laser focus is really important because what happens with it, with everybody else in the room is very important. They need to know, like you were saying, that it's going to be okay, that there's nothing bad happening here, as you said, Linda, this is the reality of life. We experience these kinds of things.

The anger one, I try to work with people to say, let's stay with this so we look at the underlying reasons why you're angry. We need to pay attention to these dynamics when they occur even if it may distract from the focus of where we thought we were going with the class that day. As you both were saying, it's so important that we do this. Usually, behind the anger is hurt; the hurt is usually about something that didn't happen somewhere else, sometimes related to somebody else in the class that happened six months ago. I once had a student cry in the last class. An African American woman, upset, owned her upset with a Latina woman who was very comfortable in the class from the very beginning. She cried and was angry at herself for having been so upset with this very comfortable Latina in the classroom. She carried it for six months. First, she got angry, and then she got hurt, and then she owned that it was really that she was jealous of this woman's ability to be so confident even though she was a first-generation immigrant from Nicaragua. Of course, there's all sorts of stuff in that, right?

The beauty of it wasn't just that they were able to embrace, but it was about multilayered experiences in that young African American woman's story that she admitted lay behind the anger. As you were saying, Linda, we cannot be afraid of conflict, and we cannot be afraid of anger. If anger happened, we've all had it, and we all know that a lot of people in social work are afraid of anger. We have to help model that it's going to be okay to engage with the conflict in the room for deep learning. Unpacking these often overly wrought dynamics is really something that we have to be able to do.

The other is the issue of fear. Fear doesn't come out often by expression; it comes out with body language and reading people's eyes. I'll give you an example. We did the film *The Thirteenth*, which is, as I know all of you know, about what's written into the Thirteenth Amendment related to not just the freeing of the slaves but the ability to re-imprison them that's built into the codification in the law. It's a very powerful and emotional film. After the film, there were people hurt, there were people angry, that was obvious. There was fear in that there were white students in particular in the room who had no idea and were afraid to say they had no idea because for other people it was so, "Welcome to my world."

There were some that were like, they didn't even know what to say, and when I see that kind of fear in two to three people, I say, "Okay, now we need small groups." I give them the question of remember the ground rules and speak to the real emotion you have, and when it's over as I walk around the group and pay attention to what's going on, I'll say to somebody, I'll say to this person, "J., what did you get from this group that you had wanted to speak about?" I know J. is the one who I perceived had fear, and he said that he "didn't know what he didn't know," and he was scared to even acknowledge this because he felt like he was being racist.

In the authenticity of his fear, as students who were angry were able to hear him, they were angry at what they've lived with for so long finally being made evident, but they could allow him to be where he was without turning it into, "How dare you be so stupid!" even though some of them still may have felt that. That laser focus in the training of myself—you know, I started out as a community organizer with the attitude of, "Let's just do this damn work." I have had to train myself to look at people and read body language and what was going on internally. Just because people weren't talking didn't mean they weren't emoting.

Kalima: I always think about strong emotions as a lot of information that we just haven't tapped into yet. I like what you said regarding when folks feel anger; it is a great opportunity, or fear is a great opportunity to say, "Well, what's the value that's attached to that?" Because there is something that you value in this moment, that the one that we have been taught to feel, these emotions—anger, shame, fear—are all emotions that we have been taught to feel at the ready. We've not been taught to go any deeper than that. So, what's the value that you have right now? If you are fearful of seeming racist, you value something in this classroom. What is it could be all about you or it could be that you have seen something new about the humanity of these people in this classroom you've never seen before, you value what you've just seen, and you're afraid to undo that. You don't even know how to bring it out.

I'll tell you, those emotions are the most fun for me because we get to really go deep. "Oh, I'm so angry." I'm like, "Okay, so many of us are angry, what is underneath that anger? What is the value attached to that anger? What is making you so angry? Because the things that you value, elicit the most emotions." I try to work with them, but I also try to do it in a way that doesn't overexpose people in ways that they're not ready to be exposed. It doesn't shine a spotlight on them in ways that they're just not ready to handle or doesn't make our space a space where we're all coming undone at the seams, and then we have no way to stitch ourselves back together in the hour and forty-five minutes that we've got.

You know, I always say feminist practice has taught me that our very strong emotions are just a bunch of information; they're not irrational, they're not stupid, it is information. You just got to get to the bottom of what it is.

Mohan: I talk about it as energy. Actually, it is energy.

Kalima: It is energy.

Mohan: Emotion, emote. I mean, there's motion right? If we block the energy ... I bring in my Buddhist meditation practice and talk about how in Buddhism and meditation practice they say, "There is no such thing as a bad thought. There is no such thing as a bad feeling." It's all information, and, in fact, it's all just flowing; everything is arising, and then it arises, and then it dissipates, and then another thing arises and dissipates, but the problem comes when we block the energy. Anger itself is not a problem, rage is not a problem, hatred, none of it is.. When we judge it and block it and then try to hold onto it, at certain times, I bring it up in that way because I do see that they really get scared, maybe not scared of feeling, but of admitting that they're feeling things.

Kalima: So true!

Guiding Principles and Strategies

The classroom is an inherently energized space. If constructed and contained correctly, students use the classroom as testing ground for self-discovery, boundary pushing, and unveiling. Emotions are a critical, necessary, and simply unavoidable part of the process. The role of faculty is to bear witness to what is being offered, prioritize the emotional needs of the student, and contain the space in such a way that the offering can be used to move the work forward.

- Principle: Handled well, students' emotional responses to difficult academic content can be a gift in the learning rather than an impediment.
- Strategy: By being prepared for such responses as opportunities for learning, a faculty member can more calmly help students both experience their emotions and through careful support, connect them to the larger content issues at hand. That person's story becomes living testimony to the larger "data" under discussion, as well as an element in healing that provides a student the chance for even greater learning throughout their lives.
- Principle: Working with emotions in academic space harkens upon feminist practice of honoring the emotions as a source of valuable information.
- Strategy: Faculty and/or facilitators who are committed to anti-racism and liberatory classrooms are charged with also examining from what political framework they are engaging their students/participants.
- Strategy: Feminist practice is rooted in principles that welcome and celebrate the presence of authentic, raw emotions. Creating a feminist space says that everyone is entitled and encouraged to express their feelings with care and recognition of privilege despite what normative academic spaces historically prescribe.

CONVERSATION TWELVE

Question: *How do you respond to these powerful social issues in research classes and in field work?*

Background to this conversation:
It is often assumed that these more socially charged topics end up in practice and policy classes alone and therefore are best addressed there, while research courses and fieldwork have "other" material to cover and therefore cannot/should not address socially charged issues.

Observations and Reflections:
In the 21st century, it seems obvious that separating out social content from other issues is increasingly impossible, because of the diverse demographics in our country, the politicized discourse crisscrossing our nation, and the inherent dynamics of power in what is deemed knowledge and how we acquire it. How can one address these issues and handle the substantive content in research as well as the large number of other competencies expected from field work?

THE CONVERSATION

Steve: Well, let me ask Linda and Mohan, both from the field and from research, how does it play out there? *How do you respond to these powerful social issues in research classes and in field work?* I see in all our practice classes why this would relatively easily happen and why even in policy I can see it happening relatively easily for other faculty. But I'm wondering, either through experiences that you've had or just reflections now, as you teach research, is emotion allowed there? Because I want to see that researchers pay attention to this and also in field work, within the field instructions, it's okay, but can they bring it to the faculty advisor easily? Is it acceptable? Do they suddenly become perceived as being a problematic student if they raise too much emotion? I just wanted to add those two things for you to be reflective about it.

Mohan: I'll definitely speak to the research part. Linda, do you want to speak to the field work part?

Linda: I want to go back to something I said a few sessions ago about the importance of building, building this into the very pedagogy, where you're redefining for the students what the norms are of what it means to learn, what learning looks like, so learning doesn't look like it's just from here up, head only. Learning does involve bringing your whole self to it; it involves taking some risks, and I have to say these things explicitly. Even to my graduate students, it's like, "Don't be focused on what do I want, how do you give me or regurgitate for me what you think I want so that you please me and get a grade." That's not education; that's instruction; that's different. If you're here to get educated, it isn't about getting the right answer; it's about taking risks, about struggling with not knowing, and raising questions more than it is about answers.

I think what I see playing out in field learning is this disconnect where we're not, as an education system, giving students the message that they need to bring this awareness of their whole self into learning, so there is this compartmentalization that happens, and they're like, "Learning happens between my ears, you know?" It's about the cognitive processes, and it's about information and regurgitating information. Then when they get to the field, they are triggered by all kinds of things.

Mohan: Absolutely.

Linda: They're like, I'm in the South Bronx; there are people who look really scary, right? They don't even know what it is; they just know they feel all kinds of things; then they rationalize, I need a field-placement change. I need a field-placement change because I think on second thought I don't want to work with homeless people, or I don't want to work with poor people, or I really am very interested in clinical work, and I was just wondering if there was a placement at an institute for me?

This really happens. That suggests that something's not happening in the classroom where they're being taught to grapple with this enough, and that concerns me for the profession. It would be like putting people in medical school and they're just kind of like, "Oh I don't do blood." It's like well …

Kalima: Just cannot do it.

Linda: This is going to be a little difficult then for you to get through medical school, right? You can see that in medical school that would probably be the response. "Well, honey, then being a doctor is not for you." But in social work school, we're like, "Oh, let's see if we can get her into a psychoanalytic institute." No, no, if you want to be a social worker, there are some things you're going to have to deal with, and yet we don't always push those things. Why? They're paying a lot of money, and you've got to keep the customer happy, and there's an unspoken pressure, the competition here in New York City with so many social work schools. We're all competing for that pool of students, so I find that to be a real challenge and a real ethical dilemma for me.

Between my commitment to what this profession is about and my belief about how we educate people in this profession and then the realities of looking at these students as paying customers who should not have to endure dealing with discomfort, that's a problem. I think this is a very real problem, and we're gatekeepers of the profession, so how responsible is it of us to go along with that and not help students really understand why they feel this discomfort when they get off the 4 train at 148th Street or 125th Street in Harlem?

Kalima: And Lexington Avenue.

Linda: How do we not, how could we not, have them deal with that? Let them graduate with an MSW, and they cannot even be in touch with the discomfort that they feel?

Kalima: One of the things I find is happening in field work, though, is that some field supervisors are not even capable of having these conversations. Sometimes I want to know, where did you go to school? Who taught you? For some folks who went to school 20, 30 years ago, maybe, I imagine they feel all this new language that new professionals are using is bull crap, and they may not take this stuff seriously and just get through the day, blah, blah, blah, and they already are sort of done with the system, just done. But supervisors who are newer emerging professionals, even 20 years out, you've got to be able to hold these complicated feelings that our students are coming to you with and engage in very deep conversations and push them to have the conversation. But the supervisors themselves are not even capable of having these conversations. They're uncomfortable. They're tired, they're spent, and some of them are not interested in any shape or form of dealing with anti-racist or anti-oppressive social work practice. That is not part of their lingo because the classroom can only do so much. Field is where the learning actually happens.

Linda: Yes, and it's where the issues really emerge like a giant Rorschach test.

Mohan: To your point about the field instructors, part of it is that we don't provide the spaces even for us as faculty and then field instructors to feel safe enough to be going to these places emotionally. I think it's a larger issue in society about even the language that we use about getting over things, a fear of really engaging with our emotions. If you look at staff meetings, how safe do we feel there, to be with our emotions? I think the students not wanting to go there is a reflection of this larger problem that we have, which is to kind of keep separating out and compartmentalizing out, and it's easier to then rationalize it. It goes back to some of the things we talked about earlier. I mean, rationalization is a wonderful defense, right? So it's easy to, in the name of academia, in the name of objectivity, in the name of all these things that are the name of …

Steve: Customer service.

Mohan: Customer service, neutrality. We then can avoid basically being with ourselves. Ultimately, I just go back to my own meditation practice, which is like you sit there, and you're like, it's so hard because you're sitting there with yourself, and you just have to be there with yourself and learn to work with it, and that's really hard …

Steve: There's one thing I wanted to say about field work before you speak about research. People in our field work office at Hunter and at the office at Columbia are now working with every student who comes in with a complaint. They're using the lessons they've gotten from anti-racism to be able to unpack whether or not they're leaving for the reasons that you were speaking about or not. They ask, "Is it really about you're not liking the placement's assignment or is it really that you're not comfortable with being at the hub in the South Bronx?"

Mohan: That's the difference.

Steve: They've worked with all the field staff, all the field directors to make that a significant part of the questions in debriefing, which then brings in the field instructor in a very different relationship.

I was very impressed with Silberman's Kanako Okuda and Columbia's Ovita Williams who have been moving field education in a very good way.

Linda: That's excellent. I'm really glad to hear that. My colleagues in field and I are also having some "see the light" conversations.

Mohan: Okay, so about research. There's a woman who wrote an article; she's actually a feminist researcher. Her name is Kristin Blakely, and I came across her article a number of years ago when I was doing my dissertation. I'll always remember her article, and it's in my dissertation. She writes about emotionally engaged research. It's a beautiful article. I can find it for us. (See Side Box 8.) It came at a wonderful time when I was doing my dissertation. I did a qualitative study, and I went through this whole pendulum swing of emotions. I went through a whole period of time where I was trying to distance myself from my emotions, and that didn't work. Then I got so swept up in my emotions that I couldn't do my dissertation. Then it was finding this balance. I was doing a topic that was very close to me, research about gay fathers.

Box 8: Emotionally Engaged Research: An Excerpt from Kristin Blakely

"Suppose we turn the focus inward, reflecting not on the research but actually on how we respond to our research, and suppose that we feel the research instead of just thinking it? Researchers' emotions are a natural part of inquiries. Taken as a whole, they are an untapped resource of information, lending insight into the research process [and] the findings of the study" (Blakely, 2007, pp. 2–3).

Anyway, through my committee, I was able to work through and get it done, but I remember coming across this article. Blakely comes at it from a feminist perspective, and she's like, we as researchers cannot separate out our emotions. In fact, it makes us ineffective. It's been awhile since I read the article, but she has this phrase. "emotionally engaged research." She basically says in research it's very easy to hide behind the veil of …

Steve: Objectivity?

Mohan: Objectivity, and even within qualitative research, which acknowledges subjectivity, we can still hide. There's a lot of hiding that happens as the researcher, we hide. We hide ourselves. We hide from ourselves in all of this. What are we hiding from? We're hiding from our emotions. She's arguing that this is not authentic, and, in fact, from a feminist perspective, research then is perpetuating a certain kind of oppression of emotion, oppression of certain ways of being. I loved what she said.

Speaking especially as a qualitative researcher, I would argue this whole notion of objectivity, even in the most sophisticated of quantitative studies, this notion of neutral doesn't exist. We don't demand of the researchers that they really own their stuff. I would argue that all researchers should own their stuff and write it, and it should be published in the articles.

Kalima: Accurately. The standpoint.

Mohan: It models, then, that we are full beings here, and that it's not a threat to the rigor of the research if we acknowledge that, and, in fact, there's ways of working with the emotions. It parallels what we're talking about with regards to teaching.

The other thing in terms of teaching research, which I've done for a number of years … , What was your question? How does emotion … ?

Steve: Do emotions, related to the question, how do they come out?

Mohan: Oh, in the research classroom?

Steve: I think you answered that question.

Mohan: Okay. I think in the research classroom I definitely encourage students to own their feelings. I use a tool called reflective diaries in teaching research, and it was actually developed by another professor where I teach. He developed this assignment called reflective diaries, where the students write these diaries after they complete each step of the research proposal in the research class. The purpose of the diaries is actually to give them a place to express all the thoughts and feelings that are coming up in the research process. Because in research, what I find is most students come into the research classroom scared, angry, anxious. Very few come in saying, I cannot wait for this class. All of them are like, oh, my gosh, I've got to take this class. They come in with all these misconceptions that it's all going to be about statistics and all this, but what this reflective diary does is it gives them a place to actually say, I hate research or I hate having to do a literature review or I feel scared, so, there's ways of working with those emotions definitely in the research classroom.

Guiding Principles and Strategies

As in previous conversations, this conversation highlights "splits" that permeate classrooms and other learning spaces—objectivity vs. subjectivity, process vs. content, emotion vs. intellect, research vs. practice. In our journeys throughout this book, we have been exploring how these splits have manifested in our personal and professional lives and have impacted the ways we approach teaching and curricula. Through dialogue with one another, we have discovered even more deeply the healing that can come from naming and challenging these splits in ourselves and in our work.

- Principle: There is no such thing as neutrality or non-social objectivity in either field work, or research. By using that awareness to guide us with the other substantive issues unique to, these areas of social work education, we deepen the learning for the student.
- Strategy: In field work, weave into discussions about practice competencies an awareness of how racism, heterosexism, and other socially charged issues may be at play in their practice.
- Strategy: In supervision, honor and normalize feelings of discomfort that will undoubtedly arise when naming issues related to race, sexuality, etc. See the discomfort as an opportunity for both student and fieldwork instructor to see each other's humanity more fully.
- Strategy: In research courses, acknowledge at the start how the entire research process is embedded within larger social forces that impact decisions of researchers, students, and faculty members.
- Strategy: Through assignments, class activities, and discussions, create venues for students to explore the role of their emotions in the research process.

CONVERSATION THIRTEEN

Question: *"THIS ROOM IS TOXIC!" What do I do when the room becomes toxic, when students of color are upset, some white students seem guilty, and others want to leave the room?*

Background to this conversation:
Almost every faculty member has had the experience of a class "blowing up," where some unforeseen incident occurs, and for some reason students respond explosively, leaving everyone overwhelmed, including the faculty member.

Observations and Reflections:
Such explosiveness rarely emerges from one incident alone. Are we able to assess not only the incident but what led up to it in ways that allow everyone to return to the classroom ready and willing to learn?

THE CONVERSATION

Kalima: Here it is—a classroom is toxic. *"THIS ROOM IS TOXIC!" What do I do when some students of color become angry, some white students seem guilty, and others look like they want to leave the room?* Who's going to start us off?

Steve: This is one question some people spoke to me about. I haven't experienced this for a long time because I've worked hard to never let things get to that point. I've reflected on it, and I think if it reaches that point, it's almost like you have to have a do-over and recognize that your class is going to have to be re-calibrated to deal with the failure of creating a learning environment to make it not toxic. I do remember this happening to me.

I've told these stories many times. Many, many years ago, this did happen to me because I was unprepared and unaware that some explosive racial dynamics actually existed between well-intentioned people.

All the stuff I've done since then to work this through, but I think for those people where this happens, the learning in this is for the teacher to say, "What is it that I have to redo in order to heal people enough to leave the classroom, so they're willing and able to come back the next week? Can I, the teacher, learn from that toxic failure what I need to do next time, hopefully by using ground rules, being able to be vulnerable, being able to model?" Learning how to model what we seek to create is tough work.

In my experience, when people have had this breakdown happen, it's when they've tried to stay with the content too much. Where earlier things have happened, and it led people to be upset, and because the teacher has then stayed with the content out of fear of engaging in this work, the students sit on it, they stew, and then later someone says something that perhaps is relatively innocuous, but the blow-up then ensues, and there's no way to put Humpty Dumpty back together again. The egg is broken at that point. (See Side Box 9.)

Then people have to say, okay, probably this would be very difficult for somebody who is content-based and afraid of vulnerability to say this to themselves, that he or she is going to have to learn from this. What are the lessons I need to learn going forward, so I don't replicate this? The anger, the hurt, the fear, and the people running out of the room are not the problem. The problem is in whatever one had failed to do earlier in that term, and overwhelmingly, it's with people trying to think content will save the day, and it cannot.

Kalima:	Let me hold up on that question until I get it right. For this question, I just name it. I'm like, Ugh it feels kind of not nice in here. I just name it.
Linda:	Hold up the mirror.
Kalima:	Just hold it up and be like, what are we going to do about it because we've got to do something about this? We cannot exist like this; what is going on? One of the things that I have done, too, is—I don't know what clinical person in the world taught me this—but this idea of a distraction, to tie in an intentional distraction, and then bring them back to the topic. I will tell them to either get up and stretch or drink some water. I kind of create my own distraction, and then intentionally bring them back to where I need to bring them back to.
	I also want to teach them to get in their bodies, too, because sometimes we feel tension in our bodies. We can feel the emotions in our bodies, and we're holding it in our bodies, and you can feel, you can see people's anxieties, and on some people it's funny but on others it's very sad.
Steve:	Why do you say that, Kalima? Why do you say that?
Kalima:	*[laughter]*

Box 9: How Emotional Explosions Happen in Classrooms

While discussing content on a policy, research, or practice question, a student or (in the workplace) colleague will suddenly explode with emotional intensity far beyond the topic at hand that easily can derail the present classroom focus on content. Instances of this have included:

- A policy discussion on welfare causes two African-American students to argue vehemently with each other over "dependency."
- A discussion on "historical trauma" impacting educational testing among some students of color causes a Jewish student to raise her family's painful history as too often ignored in classroom discussions.
- A discussion on academic standards triggers an angry outburst from a rurally raised white student who was rejected from the school's program the first time he applied.

Steve: I'm pressing my arms close to my chest. (*Everybody laughs.*)

Kalima: Or you see people's leg just start to shake and you're like, oh, boy.

Linda: Shaking the leg.

Kalima: It's funny, because I'm in a position of power, and I'm not. I'm feeling it, but I'm not feeling it the way they're feeling it sometimes. I'm like, "You know what? I think you all need to get up and stretch or something; let's stretch." I'll put some Janet Jackson on and just let them stretch and then say, "You all need to go drink some water; let's drink some water." Sometimes, I let them leave the room, but most of the time I don't let them leave the room because I want them to feel all uncomfortable with one another and look awkward and look dumb as they're trying to, you know, stretch it out and drink water, and they're drinking water and looking over at each other like, you know? Then I just bring it back.

Steve: Sharing any water bottles? (*Laughter.*)

Kalima: And then I just bring it back. I'm like, "Okay, so let's keep it 100, let's keep it real; it is really tense in this space, so what are we going to do about it?" Then I sit down because if I am leading, then I'm not teaching them to bring in those group-work skills, like we need to teach the group how to move themselves forward and not have me in power always moving them forward. Again, I wonder what parts of my identity allow me to do this or allow me to be silly and not give a damn about what they have to say about me.

Mohan: Not just your identities as you're talking, it's also your own—what's the word?

Kalima: I will tell you I cannot live in tension; I cannot exist in tension. If it's tense, I have to say something, so part of it is my own stuff. I'm working out my own stuff with them. Even if we are disagreeing, I cannot stand you, you know something like that? At least if we did that, at least we know that is what's happening.

Mohan: You want to name it.

Kalima: But I cannot. It makes me feel uncomfortable.

Mohan: As you're talking, Kalima, I'm thinking about situations that have happened.

Kalima: I want you to know that I'm just saying in the classroom you have those feelings towards students and other people in the classroom, or even in a workshop, you're just like, ugh.

Kalima: It's better for us to figure out a way to get that out.

Mohan: To name it.

Kalima: So that we can work with it.

Mohan: Also, the other part of it that comes in is our own defenses, our own styles, our defensive styles. I know for me, whenever there's tension, it could be between family members or it could be in a group of friends or it could be just between two random people in the street or in my classroom, I feel responsible. It triggers the feeling of guilt that I'm responsible somehow for the couple arguing on the street, and that is because of my own history.

In the classroom when that comes up, my initial reaction of guilt has been changing lately. Something seems to have clicked, but it's been changing where I'm not feeling as guilty, where I did something wrong and so this or that happened. I remember a few years ago, I was teaching a human behavior class. Looking back, I think I let some things go, which ended up creating a sense of unsafety by the time we got to the second semester. Also, I think I was teaching the whole thing by focusing too much on the content and not enough on the process. Then it kind of erupted in a way in the second semester, and some students really challenged me and told me specifically things that I was doing or not doing that promoted a sense of unsafety, and it was really hard to hear that, very, very hard. I was going to quit teaching. I was like, oh, my gosh forget it. How could I have let that happen? I did something wrong. That's kind of the unhealthy way to respond, which is to take on the responsibility, which is not really modeling, let's create this together.

Linda: I think the mirroring is really important, the naming it, the acknowledging it. Communicating a sense of comfort, which is "this is uncomfortable but we can figure it out. We can handle it." We can figure this out, and then probably modeling, taking the risk of sharing, of disclosing, it feels like this to me, and then encouraging other people to share as well. I think that reminds me a little bit of a field experience. It is an experience, in community context, the community being that classroom, that's triggering a set of emotions. What are we going to do? What are you going to do? That's what we want students to be able to do in the field, and they clearly are struggling with that, struggling with naming it, acknowledging it, and they are giving into their first inclination, which is to flee rather than to engage, so I think it's a real teachable moment for the students and for the professor as well because, as a member of that community, we have a responsibility. Not all the responsibility, but we have a responsibility there.

Steve: That's great, we got a short question for once.

Kalima: You think so? We have to let it marinate. *(Everyone laughs.)*

Guiding Principles and Strategies

Social issues and dynamics of oppression are at play in the classroom and not just the community. The classroom is a microcosm of society. We need to recognize this and prepare for these issues to come up.

- Principle: Faculty must be willing to recognize these issues early on and hold a mirror for whatever happens as a part of larger societal dynamics and thus valuable for us to all to learn from.
- Strategy: Besides the ground rules being posted weekly, faculty must not let little incidents slip by early in a class and think that they can be glossed over through later content. Without dwelling on them in dramatic fashion, they need to be raised with compassion and calmness as lessons for everyone to reflect on: Why was someone who spoke ignored? Why do, some students have the ease to speak often and others choose not to? By normalizing these tensions as necessary parts of the learning, you preclude the later toxicity that may otherwise occur. Principle: Underlying social tensions, if evoked in a classroom or agency, breed toxins in the body that, if ignored, cause either later physiological damage to the person or re-emerge later as harmful to classroom learning.
- Strategy: Model for students how this discomfort occurs by holding up a mirror—pausing and highlighting dynamics that occur between two or more people—and how it is necessary to resolve these dynamics sufficiently to limit personal and classroom damage. Model this through examples from your own experience—where ignored or buried, it later hurt, and, if possible, where a more engaged, vulnerable approach reaped dividends. (Once you learn how to express them, these stories do not take hours to tell; they are, however, invaluable minutes of great impact.)

CONVERSATION FOURTEEN

RESPONDING TO THE ONGOING TENSIONS OF THE 2016

PRESIDENTIAL ELECTION AND BEYOND

Question: *How do we respond to the ongoing tensions of the 2016 presidential election and beyond?*

Background to this conversation:
For most social work professionals, the surprise election of Donald Trump as president of the United States in 2016 has forced a profound reassessment of assumptions on not only race and class, but on our own failures to address powerful issues at play with large sectors of the American population.

Observations and Reflections:
For educators and other progressive social workers, with this new political environment comes the jarring realization that large numbers of the American population reject our assumptions about the focus of anti-oppression and anti-racist work. What have we failed to address for white working-class people without denying our commitments to anti-racist and anti-oppression work?

THE CONVERSATION

Steve: The question for this conversation is, *How do we respond to the ongoing tensions of the 2016 presidential election and beyond?*

Box 10: The Head is Interchangeable, the Face is Interchangeable

What is meant by a "contest of ideas" when considering the 2016 presidential election?
Separate from the debate about the role of government, foreign affairs, and the free market—which were not topics of our conversations— the content of ideas that took place that we will need to address going forward includes:

- Whose voices and stories matter as we address inequality?
- How can we speak to economic inequality that impacts everyone without ignoring historic injustices impacting people of color, LGBTQ people, and women?
- How do we show respect for others' difficult lives while confronting openly racist comments, including fears of immigrants and ignoring past and present racial injustice?
- How do we demonstrate respect for another's religion without diminishing our own beliefs?
- How do we confront what we may perceive as "alternative facts" without demonstrating condescension and elitism that dooms long-term dialogue?

Linda: Something I said to my class was that I wanted us to focus not on the person of Donald Trump but on the contest of ideas. What were the ideas that this election was about? What were all the issues that this election was about? It's very challenging. Many people feel provoked by the person of Donald Trump. I said this is the head that these ideas have on it today, but the head is interchangeable, the face is interchangeable. The ideas have been with us for a long time, so let's get in touch with what those ideas are, so that we can have a conversation about those ideas. (See Side Box 10.)

One strategy is to take it out of the individuals who are running in this election and to focus on the ideas, the ideas people voted for, or against.

Steve: This is a really wonderful question that you raised, Linda. In some ways, everything we've talked about in this guide so far, and everything that we have attempted to do in our work lives is in that question. We're now challenged by this to still live with what we've talked about in this new political setting. In particular, this idea that you mentioned, Linda, "If they go low, we go wherever we go." Historically, as you were saying, this has always meant that, in particular, people of color and other oppressed people have to always go high in response to the low road, talking in terms of violence, marginalization, oppression, indifference, failing schools, coupled with an unwillingness to correct those things, that people stand higher even in the midst of those terrible affronts.

The challenge in this is that many people who come out of oppressed backgrounds—and a lot of others, too—are going to see this election as very, very low. How can we create an environment that nevertheless allows them to be where they are with however they feel, without disregarding that obviously there are a number of working class white people who have felt left out of the national conversation.

I'm very aware that the four of us have in particular a unifying quality, which is we're all New Yorkers who have worked on anti-oppression material almost all our adult lives, and we're going to have to be aware and respectful that a lot of this country is not where New York is, and we have lessons to learn in this, too. I know I'm going to have to struggle even harder to remain open to a variety of positions I'm not used to.

There are going to be some people rightfully angry at having to be perceived as going high when there's no reason for them to do so at all. Black Lives Matter and the issues that led to its creation are not over now regardless of whoever has been elected to a higher office. The reality of those kinds of deaths and the kind of fear that, in particular, young men of color who are African American or Latino have to carry with them, and some LGBTQ people and women have to carry with them, every day is still real. Now anyone who looks like a Muslim or wears a burka feels targeted, too.

The anger that may emerge about having to pay attention to white working class invisibility or perceived invisibility and perceived indifference from social work and other academic conversations is one that's going to take a lot of work by all of us. We have to be able to allow that upset, and we have to make sure that we begin to think about how to address these conversations about why white people, white working-class people, feel disenfranchised.

The answers we have are going to relate to social class, they're going to relate to misperceptions about who really is on their side, and eventually to unpacking and dealing with how white supremacy has damaged white people with the illusion that somehow they're special and also left out of the dominant discourse in America, that their racial specialness allows them to seemingly have a better life when in fact their lives are deeply constrained and filled with unhappiness, not because of people of color, but because of social class issues and wealth inequality and privileged class access that they're not able or willing to recognize. We have to struggle with that.

Kalima: This has caused me to reflect on my experience in the military, particularly around who's in the military and at what class level they are. My first encounter with poor white folks was in the military. There's a large majority of folks in the military who are just poor and white, and this was their only option. Then you have a subset of the folks who are commissioned officers who went to college.

That experience was very interesting because the poor white folks almost seemed like aliens to me. I had never interacted with that. The only interactions and the only thing I knew of white folks was privileged white folks who had an economically stable if not abundant life. Interacting with poor white folks who I, on some levels, arguably was more educated than because I was educated in New York City and in a specialized high school, I was more educated than them, was currently in college, and that was a very interesting dynamic.

I was also in the Judge Advocate General's (JAG) Corps. I was a paralegal and came into contact with a lot of the poor white folks who were channeling through the justice system in the military. Then I circled around to being in the academy with poor white folks, but you don't know they're poor white folks because they get to come to New York, they get to assume a different identity. They get to wear the institution's sweatshirts, but when you start to get into the real stories, these are the stories.

These are the people who were from Kentucky and West Virginia, who have family members who are OD'ing on meth, but there's no space for them to have that conversation because the conversation is always about what is being done to people of color, and the case studies are always about people of color. I am not saying this isn't important. What I am saying is there are a lot of stories left out. In these spaces, I reflect on several books that helped me to understand. One, there's a book called *The Color of Wealth* that really helped me understand how class was created in America. I took parts of the book and, just like *The New Jim Crow*, focused on the policy issues, the political decisions that were made, Reagan, Nixon, to create this class divide when we were supposed to be coming together—poor white folks, people of color—to push for economic equality and equity, how that undermined that and how a lot of people were complicit in that with the hopes of upward mobilization. *Class Matters* by bell hooks, among many things, talks about poor white folks and how we don't pay attention to them.

In my classroom, I am sitting with all this knowledge, and I'm sitting in a space of how do I have a conversation about poor white people without seeming like I'm a sellout because I want to shine light on what's happening in these parts of America, and also ask for people to at least consider being compassionate or understanding or where is our common ground because there was a time when we did have common ground.

The other thing that was amazing in my development was the book *To Kill a Mockingbird*. That book talked about the Southern, white, uneducated poor class, and the ways in which they were hell bent on standing above and beyond black folks in the south. I was standing with all this in the classroom, and I'm looking at my students, and I'm trying to figure out how do I have this conversation knowing all that I know and knowing that the black students are looking at me with this expectation that I need to handle this correctly.

The radical white liberal students want to disavow the pain in some of the community, these communities, the same communities they come from, because they want to see more in alignment with progressive liberal politics. Then there's white folks who have no clue because they don't know people of color, and they damn sure don't know any white poor people.

They don't know people of color because we are segregated and all live in the same communities. But they don't care to know poor white folks. We know that by the name that we call poor white folks. We call them white …

Mohan: White trash.

Kalima: … trash.

Mohan: It's a horrible term.

Kalima: How do I hold that? Recently, things literally blew up in the classroom. The students challenged me, like, "Why are we talking about all these poor white folks, who cares about them?" Their argument was, "Look at white privilege." I said, "On some levels, yes, they're white people, which has served them, but on other levels it has not served them." This paradox is exactly what makes us angry and what makes them angry but also makes rich white people look down on them because the construct is set up for white people to win, and they're still not winning, so they are trash. For some rich white folks, it's like, "We won't even look at you." The worst thing you can call poor white people is white trash. "You are disgusting." I ask, Can we see any common ground in that?

Mohan: Yes.

Kalima: Absolutely. Absolutely, but do you see the way this was all set up?

Linda: Mm-hmm *(affirmative)*.

Kalima: I said to them, "I'm not asking you to not be angry; in fact, let's talk about your anger. Let's let it out. Let's just have a conversation about it. I'm not asking you to be Kumbaya, no. I'm asking you to be critical, and I'm asking you to privilege your humanity in this because when you privilege your humanity, it allows you to enter into a space even momentarily to see someone else's humanity and to see what parts of this that are valid and what parts of it we can let go of." I don't know if we need to go high. I don't know if we need to go low. We just need to go deep within and be honest.

Steve: Keep going.

Linda: I think that's part of the conversation we want to have. I think we literally want to frame it as "when they go low, we go … ?" and let people have a conversation about what they think, where they think they need to go, right? Part of what is needed at this point is the art of discourse around these issues.

Kalima: Mm-hmm *(affirmative)*. To dialogue.

Linda: We need to think about how to facilitate those kinds of dialogues. We need to think about where beyond the classroom those dialogues can happen and how we contain it in a way where it doesn't devolve or break out into race or class warfare in the classroom but still be able to contain the ideas. I feel like that's part of the challenge for us as social workers. That's part of the work we have to do. Before we could even get to solutions, how do we have conversations about this? How could we ever engage in a process about addressing challenges when we don't have the skills to have the conversation?

Now we have to have the conversation because these thoughts have come flying out of the closet. They are not underground anymore. They're not in the closet. They are out. They are loud. They are proud. They feel completely entitled to say what they are, so we need to think about how we're going to facilitate those kinds of conversations. That's one challenge I think for us as a profession.

Steve: What you just said was terrific. It helped me think of two questions that I think can help facilitate this, which is around keeping the dot, dot, dots going. One of those questions is that related to all of this, can we have a discussion about what "privilege" means for the white person, driving from their 7:00 to 11:00 job, to their security job, and not ever worrying about being stopped. However, they are deeply worried about their rent and whether they'll have enough food on the table. How exactly are they privileged?

Then the other question that also has to be asked in the same group is why is it that the person who is a middle class woman or man of color who's black or brown or Latino, as they're driving from their job as a professional social worker, or a doctor, they're pulled over simply because they're driving while black or brown. Why is a middle class, professional person of color being stopped for no reason at all? Those two questions are ones that need to be in the classroom at the same time.

Linda: Yes. It just brings it home.

Kalima: I'm writing this down.

Steve: Then you can take what I said and go with it wherever you want.

Mohan: It needs to be asked in the classroom.

Steve: What Linda had said triggered me in a good way. It stimulated those two possible questions, to create the necessary dot, dot, dot and about where to go—all of us, students and faculty. We are going to have to deal with these very, very hard competing truths. Can people acknowledge the truth in each story, without believing that they're canceling out their own? That is the hardest thing of all for everyone.

Kalima: People think it's zero sum.

Mohan: Yeah. That's hard.

Steve: Any educator, if he or she is going to raise both those questions at the same time, has got to be prepared; people are going to have a real hard time because they're going to be afraid that their story is lost. You know why? Because each of their stories has often been denied.

Linda: Mm-hmm (*affirmative*). What do we lose? What do people lose by seeing the commonality with each other because there is a loss.

Mohan: By seeing the commonality?

Linda: Yes. If I recognize that I have something in common with that person who's driving from the 7-Eleven, there is a loss, and that person is going to experience a loss by seeing something in common with me, right?

Mohan: That's a great question about the loss. I was just thinking as you were talking about the humanity, the shared humanity, I think the thing that comes up for me and throughout these conversations is that I often link issues around race with issues around sexual orientation because that's my reference point mostly. Vivienne Cass talks about sexual identity development and specifically around gay and lesbian people and the stages of development. (See Side Box 11.)

Like any stage theory, it can be critiqued, and it doesn't apply to everybody. There is some value in Cass's model, and she talks about the initial stage of denial. You move from a denial of oneself to a state of confusion to a state of finally acknowledging who you are but then realizing that you're different from the dominant hetero-sexual world. In that stage then there's often kind of an experi-ence of, "It's us versus them."

When you are oppressed and dis-criminated against by the larger heterosexual order it is "us versus them" because it's a threat. There is a need to say, I am against every-thing heterosexual; it's gay versus straight basically. It's the way the world is constructed in my mind. Then you move onto a further in-tegration of your own sexual identity within yourself, and in that, I begin to realize that I actually can find a commonality with the heterosexual world, and it actually doesn't take away from my gay identity.

Cass talks about this as evolutionary stages that can happen over a lifetime. We go back to earlier stages,

Box 11: Vivienne Cass on Sexual Identity Development

- Based on her clinical work with lesbians and gay men, Cass proposed six stages of developing a gay or lesbian identity: identity confusion, identity comparison, iden-tity tolerance, identity ac-ceptance, identity pride, and identity synthesis.
- These stages are not linear and are often overlapping and represent a person's journey towards integration and belonging within oneself and one's environment.
- Cass (1984) describes identity as "organized sets of self-perceptions and attached feelings that an individual holds about self with regard to some social category ... the synthesis of [one's] own self-perceptions with views of the self perceived to be held by others" (p. 110).
- This is only one model: It is important to remember that the idea of sexual identity may not resonate or be relevant for everyone.

and like any stage theory, it's not linear and all that. I think because of my spiritual practice and meditation, I keep coming back to compassion and your question about what do I lose. I'm beginning to become more compassionate toward people who are homophobic. I actually really want to sit down with a person who is deeply homophobic and really try to understand the homophobia. Part of it is my evolution with my own parents who have struggled with my coming out. I've started to begin to feel a lot of compassion for the struggle they've gone through of having a gay child.

I'm at a place where I'm curious. In a way, I'm almost more interested in talking to the person who is anti-gay. I want to try to understand where that is coming from.

Steve: How would you bring anti-gayness into the classroom?

Mohan: How do I bring that into the classroom?

Steve: The idea of something that intense into the classroom. I'm not saying you can't, I'm just not sure.

Mohan: I think I have to because of where I am at in my life. Much of the way I live my life right now comes back to my meditation practice, which is about curiosity. When we become curious about our own hatred and other's hatred, when we become curious about the things we think are wrong, the only thing that's lost is our desire to hold onto things so we let it happen. We accept.

It's not that we accept it as right or wrong. We accept it as part of what's emerging in the moment. If it comes up in the room, how do I then as the instructor be with it? I keep telling my students, "Come back to curiosity." Come back to curiosity because the mind has the tendency to want to create answers for things. We tend to want to create answers in ways that are just dichotomous.

It's either this or this, right or wrong, gay or straight, black or white. I said that type of thing perpetuates the problem. Because of the nature of the mind, the mind categorizes things. What can we do to let go of that to some extent and then ask a question? I tell them turn it into a question. Turn anything, any judgments you have, turn it into a question.

Steve: That's beautiful.

Mohan: Now the critique of that is meditation practice doesn't really look at the social order of things; it doesn't look at the political environment; it doesn't look at histories of oppression. We are talking on probably the most micro level possible, which is working with the internal workings of the mind.

Linda: There is a principle there, which is seek, with genuine curiosity, to understand the perspective of the other person, right? I think that becomes a principle that we are recommending here.

> *Come back to curiosity. With genuine curiosity seek to understand the perspective of the other person.*

Mohan: Yeah, and it's hard. Like I said, I want to talk to people who really have a hard time with two gay men adopting a kid, for example, because I also know what it feels like to feel marginalized as a gay person, but I don't know, though. It's not fair of me necessarily to ask that of somebody, like to ask a black student, saying, "Yes, find out why that white person thinks you are whatever." That's not fair of me to ask of anybody because this is part of our own development.

Kalima: Journey.

Linda: We are saying that's the dialogue that's needed, right? It doesn't mean an individual black student has to go up to a white student and say, "So tell me what's your thing with black people?" But these are the conversations that we as educators have an obligation to encourage, to encourage conversations where we seek to understand each other and each other's perspectives.

Mohan: If I'm the black student, and you are the professor, I'm going to critique my own approach here. It's easy for me to say, having lived whatever I have lived, to be at that place. I wasn't at this place. If you asked me a few years ago, I'd say I hate all straight people. What do I say to that black student or if I'm the black student? This goes back to your question of, How do I get past the feeling that I am losing something? Am I condoning this person's racism by becoming curious?

Steve: We talked earlier about standards and the importance of responsibility to a certain standard. I think in order for us to be able to expect students to do this, given this dot, dot, dot period of time that we're going to be living with for a number of years, we have to struggle ourselves to become curious and ask the questions that we really don't want to ask.

Linda: Exactly.

Steve: I still struggle with a lot of judgment related to this. I know that once again, I'm going to have to do a lot of humbling work internally to be able to arrive at being able to ask that kind of question that I put out earlier on driving. One of those questions I could have asked easily, but asking the other one, the first one, is a harder question to ask because that's not me.

Mohan: The one about the white … ?

Steve: About the white guy, how privileged is somebody going from their 7:00 to 11:00 job, to their security job and having no …

Mohan: Why is that question hard for you?

Steve: It's not now, but many other kinds of questions are. How could people vote for somebody who openly is misogynistic? How can somebody vote for somebody who openly has said that Muslim people are dangerous or that Mexicans are rapists? I have to work very hard to turn that into a curiosity, and yet, given what we've talked about, I have to take responsibility that I'm not making that attempt. If I'm going to ask that black student to answer question one or that White student to answer question two. We can't ask them to answer those questions if we're not willing to take on the responsibility and the struggle to be able to do it. I think the opportunity we have to be in the classroom is one where this responsibility is. Maybe it's more present than it's ever been. It was easy when everything was all about what the four of us already agreed with. This one is a lot tougher, and yet we've got to take it on, too.

Linda: I think this election is the result of a backlash, not only against all things we just spoke about, but also against complexity. You were talking, Mohan, about we need things to be like, "It's this or that."

Mohan: You bet.

Linda: If you think about the way the campaign played out, it was like, there are these bad people, right? Then there's these good people, and it's time for the good people to win over the bad people, and people bought that. They bought into that totally because it took the complexity of the problems we have as a country, the complexity of trying to deal with so much diversity, and it just boiled it down to what's comfortable and familiar. The other thing I was just going to say, in terms of the question, what gets lost when you try to find commonality with the other is shared commonality translates into loss. If I share a commonality with you, I lose my superiority because by joining with you now, I have to get off my perch, the perch I believe myself to be on. You lose your superiority. You also lose your identity.

Kalima: As what?

Linda: As whoever you think you are.

Mohan: Do you see those losses as a ... How do you see those losses?

Linda: I think they cut to the very core. They cut to the very core of us, right? Losing your identity is losing yourself, and ...

Mohan: Do you see those losses as beneficial?

Linda: ... and losing your superiority, I mean especially when you're slogging from your job and K-Mart and go into the 7-Eleven, it's kind of like, I've got to have something. There's got to be something that is superior about me, and I've got to be better than somebody, and at least I'm not brown.

Kalima: Exactly.

Linda: He may be the president of the United States, but he's still a black man, and I'm still a white person, and that's superior.

Kalima: Although they don't have access to that power per se, but if their relative life is not … , They don't have access to the power, but the absoluteness of this country says that because they are white, they're inherently better than.

Linda: That's right.

Mohan: That's what I was thinking about, that shared commonality. I'm saying that it's done well all within the context of privilege, so that loss you're talking about, the loss of identity, or loss of …

Linda: Superiority.

Mohan: Superiority. It's like the consequences of the loss are going to be different depending on how much privilege I already have in the society.

Linda: Loss, even if it's just perceived, even if there is no literal consequence, I just think we can't move forward in the work if we don't have people examine and acknowledge the feeling of loss.

Mohan: That becomes part of the conversation everybody is talking about, the black student and the white student, and they both talk about the loss.

Steve: Right because we also have to consider—and this is where I know the struggle would be as well, for those of us in the bubble—how do we find the humanity in the person living out in the valley in Ohio where they're just getting by day by day? Maybe they've got a cousin who's an opioid abuser.

Linda: That's right.

Steve: They themselves have five kids, two jobs, and blah, blah, blah. Where do we find our ability to say, "I see that person is having a lot in common with me"? That's going to be very hard because, what's the problem? They're still saying, "Hey, when you leave, you're still a (fill in the blank)." You're a doctor whatever. (I don't like saying the "N" word.)

Anyway, that ability to admit that even a little change inside yourself is really hard. Likewise for working-class white people to change and acknowledge the level of oppression that's existing in this country, where the deep humanity and goodness of a people is being denied or made invisible. Everybody's going to have a huge amount of risk here about giving up something that we've all needed in particular ways to hold on to, to avoid finding the mutual humanity in our American history. For once, we would be seeing us together, and that's not going to be easy.

Mohan: No, but the giving up is what's necessary, right? I relate a lot back to my meditation teachings, that actually peace comes from dropping things. It doesn't come from creating things, it actually comes from dropping all of these things, so, I think the conversation is about that. What are all the feelings that come up from dropping that?

The fear and the pain and the anger, everything that comes up from that. But I don't know because the things that we create and construct are the things that are dividing us. I remember Audre Lorde's beautiful quote: "It's not differences that divide us; it's the meaning we give these differences."

Kalima: Yes!

> "It is not our differences that divide us. It is our inability to recognize, accept, and celebrate those differences."
> — Audre Lorde

Mohan: Also part of it is, I think there's a misperception or maybe there's a fear that if we talk about our shared commonality, we give up differences. I don't think that's what it's like is this notion of, "Let's treat each the same. Let's all be the same." That is not about giving up differences; it's about not needing to hold onto it as much.

Kalima: The other thing I see in the classroom is—and I'm just going to speak specifically for people of color and about people of color because, first of all, holding onto this anger is not good, and it also can have physical debilitating effects on us. What I always say to them is, I'm not pushing you to find humanity in this because I want you to be above the fray. I don't want you to succumb to politics of respectability or you've got to be higher than anybody. It's not my place to say you've got to be walking in this Christian faith stuff. Instead, I am asking you to do it because you have to value the body that you're in, and know that holding onto anger really has a physical, mental, psychological impact.

Mohan: Effect.

Kalima: Yes. On some levels, anger materializes in your life in very simple and very real ways. What I find is that, that part of the anger that I see in folks of color who are in this work is an affirmation of their identity. If I'm not angry anymore, then what am I? Because part of my anger is because I have finally realized that I am valuable, I am worthy, I have fought hard.

Mohan: The anger is necessary.

Kalima: Right, and anger is just another way of the affirmations. So much of the anger is connected to our subjugated identity. There's a part of you, a little, tiny part of you that would want to fight every battle, even when you shouldn't be fighting that battle, because fighting the battle is the affirmation of your identity, that you work so freaking hard to come into, to love, because people of color don't automatically love that. We don't come out of the womb loving that. We come out of the womb loving ourselves. By the first grade or kindergarten, we've got all kind of issues with ourselves.

Mohan: Yes.

Kalima: The mere act—I've got this tattooed on my arm because I've got to remind myself that radical self-acceptance is my everyday work because I live in a world …

Mohan: Yes, it's an everyday.

Kalima: … that is constructed to tear me down and create a counter-narrative of my inherent truth and value. Every time I'm in that situation, all I have to do is just look down. This is my job. For some folks, their job is to be angry because the anger represents this.

Mohan: Understood.

Kalima: How do we reconstruct? What does it mean to value yourself, to love yourself, and to know that there are multiple ways of expressing that and, it doesn't always have to be anger? You don't always have to be angry in the classroom. You can be smart. You can be witty. You can be savvy. You can cut people down with your words, your eyes, your dance, your looks, your hips. You can show up so many different ways that allow for dialogue while still holding onto who you are because you don't lose yourself by not being angry.

Mohan: I definitely relate to this, but I'm a big proponent of anger. I think we get scared of anger because we may think anger equals destruction. Anger is necessary; I just want to put that out there. I'm able to talk about these things right now because I've spent many, many, many years angry.

Kalima: Right. I do think that that is involved, yes.

Mohan: I needed to give myself a space for that anger. I'm thinking about students. In one of our earlier conversations, I think I said that no emotion is bad, right? When we were talking about strong emotions in the classroom, I think that was last night, I think students come into the classroom—because again of the way we've been socialized in society, thinking in terms of right and wrong, good and bad, this emotion is good, that emotion is bad, his is good, that's bad—then also the classroom itself becomes this place where we have to hide certain parts of ourselves and show other parts of ourselves. It's about embracing all that.

Linda: Let's just say that I agree that there may be people who are at a point where it's appropriate to think about not letting the anger be so dominant, that it affects health. I think there are others for whom part of the process is getting angry, so I just want to be careful not to shut it down.

Kalima: Right, totally not, because we talked about racial-identity development yesterday. Anger is part of the racial-identity development process. It is completely part of it. Again, I'm going to tell you, when people are not pushed to move beyond that anger, it materializes. It manifests itself in the body.

Mohan: In the body, yes, it does.

Linda: Yes, and it's destructive.

Kalima: Right? What is the role of modeling something that holds the "both and." That's why I said in my class, "You're angry; let's talk about." Then where is the next step?

Mohan: It's holding onto it and not expressing it—that's the problem.

Kalima: Right, exactly.

Mohan: When we have anger, and we don't express it, it has no place to go. The energy gets lodged in the body, and we get sick.

Steve: Wow, I think there's a lot of "dot, dot, dot" in our future about where we go, which is why this conversation will repeat itself many, many times.

Linda: Can I add just one more thing to that? For us as professors of color, when we introduce or facilitate these conversations, there is the question of, "And who are you to introduce this conversation?" Right?

Kalima: Mm-hmm *(affirmative)*.

Linda: If I am that person who's driving from K-Mart to 7-Eleven, maybe I don't feel comfortable talking about that with you as the instructor in the front of the class. You fell off the affirmative action truck, and now you're up there while I'm schlepping from K-Mart. I've got to get out of this class to get to K-Mart then get to the 7-Eleven, and then write a paper for you.

Kalima: Right.

Linda: Okay, and that shit is going to come up.

> *If I am that person who's driving from K-Mart to 7-Eleven, maybe I don't feel comfortable talking about that with you as the instructor in the front of the class. You fell off the affirmative action truck, and now you're up there while I'm schlepping from K-Mart. I've got to get out of this class to get to K-Mart then get to the 7-Eleven, and then write a paper for you.*

Kalima: Yeah, I think we've talked a little bit about this—the class stuff that comes up earlier.

Linda: The affront that you could be in that position.

Kalima: Exactly.

Linda: The affront that I have to call you "doctor."

Steve: We just all have to be ready for all that comes because it's definitely coming.

Linda: It's coming.

Steve: A whole bunch of trucks.

Linda: Good. Let's hope we're ready!

Guiding Principles and Strategies

Regardless of one's position on the outcome of the 2016 presidential election, the results signal a need for a profound reassessment by professionals in both social work and education regarding what we have failed to incorporate into our curricula and what we need to maintain. Holding both parts of that assessment will be an important guidepost for us over the coming years.

- Principle: Anti-oppression work can no longer ignore issues of social class alongside issues of race, homophobia, and sexism. This effort will require an openness to new ideas and perceptions of the world that require us to use the other pedagogical principles expressed in this guide.
- Strategy: Recognize your great internal effort to hold "multiple truths" of different perceptions of social reality that will challenge language and concepts of privilege, power, and positionality. Make sure classroom ground rules have prepared both you and your students to respond to what initially may be highly conflictual discussions.

PART THREE: SHIFTING THE TEACHING PARADIGM

CONVERSATION FIFTEEN

Question: *What are the consequences of faculty of color raising issues of race knowing that data shows programs inconsistently support these efforts?*

Background to this conversation:
This questions springs from the dilemma faculty of color as well as LGBTQ faculty face if they consistently raise concerns about these social issues. On the one hand, these issues matter greatly to them and often animate at least part of their work. At the same time, they worry about being labeled "a race person" or "only concerned about LGBTQ issues."

Observations and Reflections:
It is clear that faculty are often identified by their area of expertise and interests: clinical work with chronic schizophrenics or leadership in nonprofit settings. They are rarely labeled as "hung up" on such issues. Is this same respect applied to those faculty committed to and as substantive on issues of race, sexuality, and class?

THE CONVERSATION

Kalima: *What are the consequences of faculty of color raising issues of race knowing that data shows programs inconsistently support these efforts?*

Listen, I'm not tenured while we're having these conversations, and I'm not on the tenure track at this point, so naturally, my relationship to evaluations and ratings is categorically different from someone who is. (See Side Box 12.) It's important for me to ground what I have to say in that truth, as to not disrespect folks.

I don't think about my anti-racism work in terms of ratings because, first of all, I'm teaching in institutions that are supportive of the work. Again,

Box 12: The Weariness of Being Wary

Stress and fatigue are no strangers to faculty.

- Systemically marginalized faculty are oftentimes intimately impacted by injustice in ways their privileged counterparts are not.
- There are few supports embedded in institutions to respond to the unique needs of faculty or otherwise, so it's critical that systemically marginalized folks prioritize self and community care.
- Systemically marginalized folks may experience a sense of misrecognition and loneliness in predominantly white institutions. Connection is central to survival. However, the act of connecting must not fall solely on the person in need. Recognition and care must be an ethic built into the culture of the institution/organization and the responsibility of all.

like I said, these institutions have said, "We know that your evaluations are going to reflect that you talk too much about race, and we support it, so we're just going to weight this differently."

There are various measures of my work that play into evaluations such as final quizzes, assignments, and the such that matter to me only so much as they relate to learning and growth.

What I am most concerned about regarding institutional support is the impact of this stuff on the bodies of people of color and how that shows up in the classroom every single day. I think about the unwritten expectation for folks of color to bring the daily news into the classroom particularly, incidents of violence against the bodies of people of color. I mentioned this in our last discussion; we simply do not get a break.

We have to talk about it with our families and talk about it again in our places of work. Then we come into the classroom and, as folks of color, there is an implicit expectation that we will discuss it again. Not only must we create space to address the latest assault against our humanity, we have to make sure that we hold the space in the right way because that, too, may show up on a formal or informal evaluation. To be honest, the critiques about times when the space was not held correctly and folks were harmed hurt the most. Please don't forget that I'm doing all this carrying, we are doing all this work while we're also hurting. Except the expectation is that we don't share in that space because it's really about the students, and if you attempt to participate in their space without the perfect balance, then they can complain about that too. I think about that, and I also think about the ways in which so much pressure is on us to get it right all the time.

When issues of race and racism come up and when we bring them up, the conversation has to be so perfect, and when it's not perfect and you're a person of color, I find that some people are so critical. I have been the receiver of scathing criticism for making a mistake, and I've seen it happen to other folks. More than anyone else, it seems as though students of color are so critical of faculty of color when we don't get it right. While I understand what this about, it still hurts because on some levels, their opinions are the ones that matter the most.

The third thing that I see—and again, I'm not only thinking about the institution's evaluation, I'm thinking about the ways the work impacts our bodies which on some levels is a form of evaluation. What I tend to see and can sometimes feel is that we're standing alone in the practice of our commitment to anti-racism work. It can become hard having to be the lone voice, to always have to bring up, "Oh, wait. There's no gender analysis in this. Oh, wait. There's no race analysis in that."

It is hard, it is scary, and it is risky. What is the role of the institution in supporting faculty beyond evaluations? What is the role of the institutions in creating spaces for us to explore our own feelings and practice, bringing these often difficult conversations to the classroom? It's upsetting.

Mohan: I think when I read this question and reflected on it, I had a hard time with connecting to it. I think part of the reason is I have a problem with the whole person-of-color paradigm. Not that we shouldn't be using it, but that I think that I get lumped in with, let's say, you. You and I, Kalima, actually don't have the same experience. I don't walk into the classroom worried that I'm going to be judged by my students based on my color.

Never in the years of teaching have I worried about students and what they're thinking of me and how they're going to rate me in relation to my color. I guess because I've never felt like my skin color or being Indian, a non-white person in this country, has actually gotten in the way of my professional aspirations.

It sucked in high school and elementary school and college. Yes, I was harassed, and teased, and there was a lot of racists. Microaggression after microaggression I swallowed, and then basically I have been in therapy for many years dealing with all that stuff. It's interesting. There's something about my professional life that has had its own momentum, and my being a racial minority in this country and a person of color doesn't even dawn on me when I walk into the room.

Other people might see me as the brown guy coming in, but I never have felt like that's been used against me, or I don't walk into the classroom or with my colleagues feeling like it's been used against me. That's why I have a hard time with being called faculty of color, even though I am a faculty of color. In ways, I think I could probably relate much more to Steve in terms of that.

I do think, though, that because of that maybe I feel colorblindness towards myself in a way. Certainly it's taken me a long time, my life, to embrace my brownness and not want to be not brown. I've come a long way with that and not feeling shame about being not white.

I think because of what I talked about there is something where I walk into the classroom, and I probably don't bring up issues of race as much as I could or ought to. I do bring up other issues and struggles. It's interesting.

I'll bring up sexuality. I'll bring up gender but around race. I think there's something in there about me not fully dealing with my experience as a person of color in the world and also realizing that it hasn't actually gotten in the way in my own mind. There's a part of me that probably doesn't bring up race and racism in the classroom the ways that I could. Maybe that has to do with some sense of privilege. I don't know.

Steve: It's interesting. Unlike the other three of us, Mohan, your experience in the classroom is you have a vast majority of black and brown, both Latino and African American and Afro-Caribbean people as opposed to all of us where there are far more white students.

Mohan: That's the other thing I mentioned. I realized that's the other piece of it. I realize that I'm working at a college where to be a white student you're different, so it's in a way already in the room so much because of what my college is and, on an institutional level, there's a real strong commitment to basically serving people of color in the Bronx.

Linda: I just wanted to reflect a little bit on what's different from your brown, and Kalima's brown, and my brown. I think that's the issue of the umbrella of people of color, and you're feeling like, "Well, I don't quite. Yes, but no." If it were just skin color, well we would be put in the same boat.

Mohan: Well, I think it has to do with the intersectionality pieces. It's about that, number one, I'm a man, and I guess I'm wondering. I don't know whether I walk in with a certain amount of male privilege not being questioned as a man. I think this comes from growing up in an upwardly mobile Indian immigrant family that was very much about higher education and career success. It relates back to the last question around class privilege and educational privilege.

I was actually just talking about this yesterday. It's not enough in my family to have a job. You have to have a career. If you just have a job in my family, there's a lot of shame around that. There was such a drive around career. It doesn't matter. Get three Ph.D.s if you want. When it comes to education, go into debt. Go into $100,000 of debt.

As Indians in this country, the brownness of an Indian, our skin color, we're both persons of color, but the history in this country being an Indian immigrant where I'm assumed to be a professional, there's an assumption of being a professional and being confident. That's the thing.

I have a very close colleague. She's a black woman, and we're on a research team together. There's two teams. One white gay man, one Indian gay man, one black female, one white female. We've got a nice mix there. Around the skin-color thing, we're both faculty of color, but around the race stuff, I'm as similar or different to her as I am with my white female colleague. I don't know if I answered your question.

Linda: I feel like you did. That makes me think that as we continue this conversation, every time we talk about color or every time we talk about race, we have to keep unpacking. What do we mean by that? Is it because we have a certain skin color? Is it a whole other perception about what that means? Is it a class issue? Is it an education issue? Is it a socioeconomic issue? What are we really talking about?

Kalima: Can I just say one thing? I agree with your line of questioning, Linda. What I want to add to your list is the different ways in which the world acts upon us as well. The other thing that I'm thinking about is, Mohan, you mentioned that your parents came here to go to graduate school.

Your parents came with status or with the promise of securing status with the acquisition of a graduate degree, and as a result, they were then able to achieve a certain level of class status—not political status, but class status versus folks who are coming from other countries where they didn't have access to education and, therefore, whose journey looks and feels quite different.

Steve: It's interesting, the example you give because in the 50s there was the Braceros Project, which purposely brought in Mexican laborers to this country to do the agricultural work. Lo and behold, the construction of a policy served very different purposes—some people are perceived as being "less than," and other people are being perceived seemingly above. That struggle perpetuates itself, which is why part of this conversation is that one can't just say, "Color is color." The construction is related to these other dimensions as well, whether it's Puerto Rican, Afro-Latina, African American, white, whatever it is. All of them have different interpretations as to what it means.

Mohan: The other thing is that I grew up in a family that always wanted to align themselves with white people. There was a sense that there was a real shame around being different from white people, and I grew up with that message, "Don't be too different," which basically means, "You need to assimilate yourself with all of the white people."

I grew up near Allentown, Pennsylvania. In my high school, out of 1,500 students, there were two black kids, maybe three or four South Asian kids, and about 20 East Asian kids, and that's it—1,480 other kids were all white and many of them with German last names. There's a piece of it that I think is still coming up for me

> *How do we "unpack"? Unpacking requires us to inquire, layer by layer, what may lie behind a comment or unexamined fact that some people take for granted while others perhaps never do. For example, some people assume being "dynamic" is only a matter of temperament. Unpacking such an assumption goes through the layers of experience and stories of differential opportunities in, say, classroom participation, expressions of humor or upset, and public speaking that can dramatically change one's interpretation of a "dynamic" speaker.*

around being comfortable as a person of color because I grew up with this message of, "In order to survive, in order to feel good about ourselves ..." and there's a long history of that because even within my family around skin tone in India, there's huge amounts of colorism where within the same family a baby is born, and the first thing that is said, "Oh, so-and-so had a baby, kind of dark."

That's the first thing that is said about a baby sometimes. The first thing. It's always so gruesome to me when I think about it, but I grew up with all of this sense of, "It's not good to be dark."

Steve: What this speaks to is this is also a place where white ally-ship has to mean something by knowing about this reality: There are going to be other struggles that people go through where some people are perceived as "less than" and are being marked down simply by walking in the room.

That's our responsibility. People who have white-skin privilege and all that goes with that have got to be willing to address this consistently in two ways. One is with other faculty, which I mentioned earlier. It's a fact. It has to be dealt with so that people of color or LGBTQ folks aren't perceived as being less than.

The other issue, though, as we've spoken about before, relates to how students are evaluating different faculty. I have the experience teaching this multi-method practice course with many faculty. It's taught by a large number of adjuncts, some of whom are younger women of color. There's a mix, but there is a significant number of younger women of color. By younger, I mean somewhere from late 20s to early 40s. Invariably, a significant number of them get harassed by students who perceive them as less capable. "You have nothing to teach me."

They don't say that, but they question their authority very early on. It's my responsibility to respond, and it's a tricky thing to do. On the one hand, I can't go into the classroom and use my authority to tell them how terrible they are because that would just lessen the authority of the teacher. On the other hand, to do nothing is to allow it to occur, and the body of that person of color is going to be that much more damaged.

We use our time together as a faculty group to talk about this, in some ways to predict it and to support people on answering it where we tell new faculty to immediately have students meet with them and/or other people in the area where we put that issue of authority and capacity to rest. We bring the issue up in large classroom settings (all the sections together). We openly confront students that they are going to have to struggle with implicit bias as to which faculty are perceived as academically capable and who is not. We discuss the racial/gender bias elephant in the room before that elephant charges in and destroys the room. If we don't raise this unsettling issue of implicit bias applied in a more generalized way early on, we always end up in trouble later on. This approach isn't ideal, but what are the alternatives?

Linda, you were saying that if you complain, and you yourself bring it up, well then, it's a complaint where you're defending yourself. It has to come from a variety of other sources where we see that it exists and rather than let people with less power carry that burden that I don't have to carry, we have to recognize that we have to pre-empt this problem from festering and then growing negatively to impact a young faculty of color.

If we're going to sustain a robust, multi-racial, multi-cultural curriculum and staff, we have to support the variety of ways in which students and all of us have to struggle with this because this conversation shows how deep this struggle can be. It's not simple. It's painful, and yet we have to step into it because the alternative is to live in the isolation of that struggle over perceptions of performance, which makes it that much harder.

Linda: I want to answer the question, but just one more reaction. My brother's skin is darker than mine. He's probably your complexion, Mohan. My mom's skin is darker than mine, but I'm blacker in my family because of my hair, lips, nose, butt. It isn't even the color.

Steve: I think you're lighter than me.

Linda: I don't think so.

Steve: Let's see here. I think it's pretty close. See? *(Walks over.)* Look, pretty close.

Mohan: Pretty close. Different tone.

Steve: I got a lot of hair stuff going here. *(Everyone laughs.)*

Linda: It isn't the color thing.

Kalima: It's the markers.

Linda: It's the markers, right. When I was born, I was very pale, and it stayed that way except when I went to Puerto Rico, and I was under the sun all the time. I had a nice color, but it is about how close you are to African features. Indian would be another category in terms of the way many Puerto Ricans that I know would describe Indian.

It would be like, "You are 'indio.' You're brown, but you're an attractive brown," because you have attractive hair texture. You have chiseled features. We have this whole distinction in Puerto Rican culture about being "chata"—wider nose, thicker lips. That's "chata" versus "perfilado," chiseled.

The more chiseled you are, the better. The straighter your hair is, the better. Indian is okay. My brother was often described by my mother as Indian because his hair was so curly but silky, and mine wasn't. I needed more work to fix me because, you know. This stuff is very loaded. It's so frickin' loaded.

Going to the question about what are the consequences for faculty of color who raise these issues, I think there are very real consequences, and I'm not even worried about the evaluations. I think the consequences beyond the evaluation are how you're perceived among your colleagues on the faculty. I've seen it in faculty meetings.

It's like, "There this person goes again. They see race issues everywhere in everything. When we talked about the color of the paint, why are you bringing that up? It has nothing to do with this." I'm concerned that professors of color will get perceived as whiners or that we're thin-skinned or bristling and reacting to things.

I'm concerned that it will take away from our credibility or what the institution seems to value. It also means that no matter how much expertise we may demonstrate in publications, or teaching, or conferences, if it's about those issues, it's just those issues. It's not as legitimate as all the other issues that people are scholars about. That I would find really offensive because it's putting you in a box. I feel like on some level you're being put in a box, but then you're told that you put yourself in the box because you kept talking about these issues.

I think that's a real danger. It means you get to be de-legitimized as a scholar, as a professional. You're a Johnny one-note or a one-trick pony. That's all you know. You're not as well-rounded or professional as the rest of us. I think there's a real risk, and you have to balance that risk with the real responsibility because you can't sit there and not bring it up.

Steve: If people want to know what they can do, white people I mean, what you're saying is approach people on lots of stuff, one of which may turn out to be about race, but the others are all about substance or related to what that person has that have nothing to do with it. The racial or social weave will happen, but if all that happens is the box, why would people ever feel safe enough to be able to break out of it at all?

Linda: Right, and you had asked me, Steve, to make the connection also to running an agency. I do recall in doing that, having to be the translator of what the young people we work with were going through. Any ED is going to have to do that, but for an audience, whether it was board members or donors, for audiences that had no real contact or connection with that world, I felt like I made that more comfortable because I represented what the young people could be if we did our work well. "Well, if we can do this right, they can be like you."

That kind of a person of color. That's what we want. This is great. This is perfect that you are the leader of this agency because you are what we hope these kids will become. I always had mixed feelings about that and felt very much like a passionate advocate and a bit like a prostitute who was ...

Mohan: Being used?

Linda: Yes, albeit voluntarily. Volunteering to be used to make our kids more palatable to people who saw my young people as quite damaged, as in, "Those are some messed up kids. Why should I give?" I had to make that case that they were worthy of investment. I used to try to say things that I thought were provocative, such as "We should have the same standards for these kids as our own kids," but it never felt provocative enough, like if I had said, "Did anybody ever have to convince you to invest in your nieces and nephews? The fact that they were human, wasn't that good enough?"

I had a donor once ask me if the place that we had renovated for our girls was too posh, that was the word, and asked if they would not keep getting pregnant to come back and live there. The only way I could respond was, "Well, were you ever worried that your home was too nice for your own kids, and they'd never leave?" I think she got it. She laughed, and she was like, "No, although there's a lot of kids, you know, on their parent's couches. Maybe that's the problem." But I said, "No. You set a standard that they could internalize and then go build a life like that. That's what we're doing here."

What you want to say sometimes is a lot less nice than that or I would say at our galas, "What you want for your kids is what we want for our kids. Same thing, one standard because they're kids." That was my idea of a political message. Kind of like I'm making a statement, but it was always conflictual. There was a part of me that felt like, "Why do I have to beg for you, for society to do what's right?" If these were little white kids, would my begging be different?

Kalima: Right. What I'm hearing you say and some of the things that happen on faculty is this need to be incredibly strategic in what we say and how we respond to these microaggressions while holding onto our integrity in that process. How do you say what needs to be said and not jeopardize that funding? You could feel all kind of ways, but people still need to open up that new housing for your girls.

I can feel all kind of ways about stuff, but my main business is to be in the classroom and to have these critical conversations with young people who are emerging as social work professionals. For me, when I'm in a crazy situation, I use a glass of water to give me some time. I'll just stop and drink just to calm down sometimes but also to allow myself time to think: "How am I going to respond to this and be honest to who I am and my fundamental core beliefs, yet is it strategic enough to get this point across so I don't completely foreclose the conversation or create a new enemy?"

That is the level of stress in my body that I'm carrying almost every day—in class or not. It's stress that other folks may not even have to deal with because there is no need for them to think about what they say. When people are levying a microaggression, they're not thinking about that shit. They're just saying, "Here's this crazy racist thing I'm going to say to you because this is what I think. I don't even know that what I'm about to say is wrong, so I'm going to say it to you," and you can be the person in power, and they're still going to say it to you.

You, as a person in power, have to think to yourself, "How am I going to respond to this in the most strategic way?" That takes a lot of energy from the body. In *Between the World and Me,* Ta-Nehisi Coates talks specifically about the body. Like so many black feminists, he talked about the ways institutional oppression acts upon the body in real tangible and less tangible ways. So much of the joys, pains, and stress are lodged, held, stored, massaged, and worked through within our bodies.

I think about all the great leaders that we lost because they held this stuff in their bodies. Audre Lorde, so young. Whitney Young, so young. So many people died unexpectedly because I believe their bodies were storing the pain of racism. The consequences are far beyond evaluations. It is the way in which it shows up in the one place we are supposed to have complete control over, our body.

Mohan: When you were talking about the body, Kalima, and then what you were saying earlier about on the one hand, you're in a box, people put you in the box, and then you're operating from this box, and you're using it strategically, then it's like, "It shouldn't have to be this way. We should be looking at humanity." I think it's bringing up a couple of things for me. One is, I hear it sometimes in the classroom and among colleagues about this gender-blind, colorblind, race-blind. Let's move beyond all of these boxes to the humanity of everything.

The thing is, the person who's saying that has the ability to say that. To say, "Oh, well. I treat all human beings the same." I come across this when it comes to LGBTQ issues when I teach about that. Sometimes you hear the statement, "Well, sexuality doesn't matter," but then it's a heterosexual person saying that. Someone who doesn't know what it's like to experience homophobia, and heterosexism, and the violence. There's this whole slippery slope around the humanity thing, which is that it erases oppression when oppression exists because we're not operating from that place.

We're not operating—as you said earlier, Steve, about the social oppression—even though I may want to from an individual perspective operate from a place where it doesn't matter what your sexual orientation is, it doesn't matter what your race is, gender is, the truth is, it's stripping everything of the fact that all of this stuff has been given meaning. That's what came up for me around what you said, and I think what you're saying around the body made me think about how I've come to a place in my teaching where—well actually not just my teaching, my life—where I can finally begin to feel my body more.

I talk to my students about it. I got this actually from couple's therapy training, that we relate to the world in four different ways: Through thinking, through feeling, through sensing, and through doing. There are these different ways that we're connecting to the world and typically, because of the way we were brought up, typically two of those ways are underdeveloped, and two of those ways are overdeveloped.

Some people were given the message when they were children, "Don't feel angry. Don't feel things," and so we end up suppressing and repressing our feelings. Then what we end up doing is overcompensating with, "You should be thinking all the time." You're a child that wants to use your body, and then you're told, "Don't be like that. That's too flamboyant. You're acting like a girl," or whatever, so then they constrict their bodies. It makes me think about the classroom and the ways that intellectualism can squash things, the ways that we can turn anything into an intellectual exercise.

Linda: Disconnect ourselves.

Mohan: Disconnect ourselves. I know that for a fact because I lived a lot of my life disconnected from the feeling part of me, the sensing body part of me, and I became one big head. What you're saying about the body makes me think about that, about how in faculty meetings, how in the classroom, as an instructor, I recognize the power I have to reframe things, to squash when there's an energy in the room. I'm thinking about bell hooks again. She talks about the disharmony that's needed in the classroom. We need to feel in the body, I'm realizing. We need to feel, and how much room within the academia and within curricula do we really give to that? To give to all the ways that we can experience the world outside of conceptually, outside of concepts. I get it, because I've had debates with faculty before saying, "This is not therapy. This is not the space for it. This is an intellectual space."

Why are we creating these splits between the knowledge that can be gained from the body versus the knowledge that can be gained from thinking about something? That just made me think about that. I don't know how it relates to this question, but anyways, it's …

Kalima: It's fun to bring up memories.

Mohan: I guess it is. What I'm hearing you say is that you want to honor that felt experience. You want to honor that, but then to bring that up, then you become that person who is the sole person who's holding all of that.

Kalima: In the classroom.

Mohan: When you allow yourself to feel in the body, you absorb the energy in the room. Then people project it. They disown their own selves, and then as the person in the room who's more open to it, you absorb all that stuff and then you go home with it.

Kalima: Yes. Sometimes when you're talking about disconnecting, dissociating, that's completely a defense mechanism. Sometimes having to make that decision and not even feeling like I have the right to make that decision because I'm a person of color, and I've got to always be in it all the time. I just think to myself, "I'm 37 years old, trying to have a child and having all kinds of problems."

How much of this is related to the work? This intense feeling all the time, when I listen to NPR, no matter what, just listening to Trump, the way in which it lodges, the anxiety lodges, in my body, and I say to myself, "Oh, you've got to let that go. You've got to go work out. You've got to eat well."

I have to do so many protective things because this world is set up in such a way that I'm always feeling attacked in some way. For me, evaluations matter, but the actual on-the-ground work has a far greater impact, but it's compounded and complicated by the evaluations system that does not look at how hard this work is on a daily basis.

Linda: I just want to thank you for raising the impact on our body because I think we don't run around really conscious or aware of it. It just is, but it is exhausting to have your antennas never relax. They're always on, like you are attuned to so many unspoken dynamics everywhere, all the time, on the subway, wherever. You step into Lord and Taylor, you just know that there is a reaction like, "What are you doing here?"

Kalima: Every day.

Linda: Those antennas never get a break. That's exhausting. Then you absorb so much toxic stuff. It is an extra burden. As though being a human being wasn't enough work, it's an extra burden to feel responsible, to see it, to catch it, to address it, address it without hurting yourself, to constantly have to prove your legitimacy, your humanity, your credibility. We do all that without having to be conscious. It's just happening all the time. You don't even have to think about it consciously. It's just what you have to do. Then deal with, "Was I protecting enough of my people? Of all the people that I represent. Have I been protective enough of them? Loyal enough to them? Enough of an advocate? Or did I just sell out to get that grant or to get that donation?"

Steve: Wow, what you both are speaking to is something we in the white, straight world almost never even consider, let alone act on: The toxicity that these daily interactions cause, and their literal impact on your bodies and your well being. I am left with both a mix of sadness for what you put up with and great respect for how you both endure and thrive. For me, it's all the more reason to work to create a world—in the classroom, in meetings, on the damn street!—where that kind of toxicity evaporates. It's not enough, but there's no excuse not to at least do that in the worlds that I am a part of.

Guiding Principles and Strategies

Leveling the playing field for all faculty in the evaluation, tenure, and promotion process requires acknowledging that none of us comes from a neutral position and that implicit bias from students, colleagues, and administrators is both advantageous and disadvantageous to certain groups. Such an acknowledgement need not be a threat; rather, it can serve as a relief by inviting junior and senior faculty, white faculty and faculty of color, straight faculty, and LGBTQ faculty to share the burden of breaking the silence on racism, heterosexism, and other social issues; so that the toxic damage done to so many is diminished.

- Principle: Senior faculty must demonstrate that academic areas of interest related to race, sexuality, and other social issues, including issues of oppression, are as substantive and valuable as other areas of expertise.
- Strategy: Faculty development activities should address these topics with full participation of all faculty, so they are not marginalized and diminished, this impacting faculty of color and other faculty's opportunities for promotion and tenure.
- Principle: To recognize that issues of social oppression that happen in society and in the classroom heighten the pressures, psychologically and physically, on faculty of color and LGBTQ faculty that other faculty do not experience.
- Strategy: While no sets of actions can fully compensate for these stressors, white, straight faculty need to consistently integrate such material into their classrooms and faculty meetings, so they are not carried by faculty of color and LGBTQ faculty. The paradoxical work here is not to normalize these issues as acceptable but to make them present so they are not perceived as the solitary responsibility of the burdened few.

CONVERSATION SIXTEEN

Question: You graded me unfairly because I am ... ?

Background to this conversation:
As we continue to assess our relationship to the term and practice of teaching, we organically move into a space of examining our relationship to the process of evaluating our students and the politically charged emotions at the center for all involved.

Observations and Reflections:
- *Council on Social Work Education (CSWE) mandates assessments of specific social work skills. While the actual assessment tool is arguably objective in nature, the issuing of grades is not for anyone involved. Faculty are sometimes ethically challenged in the assessment stages of learning, and students whose main source of self-concept may be stemming from academic success are equally challenged.*
- *The assessment stage of learning may present some additional challenges for faculties of color and those with systemically marginalized identities. There are pre-established standards, unspoken expectations, implicit bias and, on the part of faculty, a pull toward solidarity that all collide to possibly compromise the integrity of the process.*

THE CONVERSATION

Linda: How do we square, how do we jibe that community that we create as professors? Where there is an exchange, you bring your lived experience, I bring mine, we make meaning of it together. How do we square that with that assessment process? The power of issuing the grade, when a student is not comfortable with the grade and feels like, "We had a connection. I was feeling you, you were feeling me, and I have an A minus, and I don't understand why there's a minus next to my A." The question becomes, *You graded me unfairly because I am … ?*

Steve: That's good stuff.

Linda: How comfortable are we where we feel like, well actually, here's a couple of A papers. This one doesn't measure up. This is really a B plus or whatever. How do we jibe that power?

Mohan: What do you mean by jibe that power?

Linda: How do we reconcile? How do we reconcile this philosophy we have around teaching, where we build community, we basically walk a set of values. We respect that everyone in the room has something to teach and contribute. We're learning from each other, but now I've got the power here. I hold your grade, and I'm the only one who can issue it, and there is an authority that comes with that, and if you're not happy with that, you still have the power. I think it can be a struggle for the students, which is, I really felt a feeling of community with you, then you flipped on me, and now you're the boss.

Mohan: I don't think it has to be mutually exclusive though. It's not to discount people's experiences, the lived experience, but there's power that has come from the fact that I've earned the degrees I have and that I've actually had the formal education that I've gained that has now allowed me to be in that position.

Linda: With building a relationship that has a tension in it, I have this authority, and we're also members of this community.

Mohan: I could reframe that as a responsibility. I would argue that in the education process, self-assessment is not enough. We need something outside of ourselves to give us the reflection back. That doesn't necessarily have to equate into a grade. It could equate into a narrative. It doesn't have to be a grade. I need, as the student, somebody outside of me to give me a reflection on my performance, on my knowledge, whatever the benchmarks are.

The way to square it then is to reframe that authority as actually the responsibility that I have. In fact, the educational process requires that. I would argue that it requires that. Otherwise, we would say that basically everybody assigns themselves their own grade, and I think there are programs that probably do that. I don't know about social work programs, but maybe there are other ones that basically say you determine your own grade.

I think that's unfair actually because how can we be objective about ourselves? I need somebody to tell me, and it could be a grade, but I like the concept of reflection. I need somebody who actually has a perspective on it based on their education and their experience to give me that assessment.

Linda: That feels comfortable to me, but I'm putting myself in the shoes of the student, who makes us feel uncomfortable. It's like the parent who is like, "Look, I'm your mom, I love you. You can tell me anything." "Okay, mom. I want to tell you I got high last night." Slap.

Mohan: Just like you're betraying them.

Linda: Right, a potential betrayal, but now I'm going to kick your ass for doing it, and because there's a responsibility I have as a mother, I have to kick your ass for doing it. It still feels, it's still experienced as a betrayal. I don't know where I'm going with this.

Kalima: No, it's a great question.

Linda: I'm wondering about that tension, and I'm wondering if there isn't more we need to do to acknowledge that tension.

Mohan: With our students.

Kalima: I think that we could build a relationship and still not … what's the word? Skimp on quality. I'm going to change that word. We don't have to compromise quality work and expectations just because we built the relationship.

Linda: Right.

Kalima: I had this very experience recently. I was committed to building really deep relationships. Somehow this equated to students' feeling like they could turn in papers late or turn in half-baked papers. I was like, "Just because I see you as a human doesn't make me any less of a human or a professional or lover of my profession. You will do this paper again, or you will just fail."

Mohan: It also doesn't make you see them as less.

Linda: The fact that they do it, the fact that they tested, that suggests there is a confusion.

Kalima: There is a confusion because they're also not accustomed to being in a relationship where I am actively diffusing power. I'm actively not being power over, and so I'm being power with, and you're confused about it because it's unfamiliar to you.

Mohan: It's unfamiliar.

Kalima: It is unfamiliar, and so just because I am honoring your humanity does not make the work of educating social worker and effective social work practice—any less important. Mediocrity is not even an option. That understanding should actually be partly essential to our relationship because that is the reason why we are in a relationship at this point. I did not meet you in a cafe. I met you in a classroom.

That incident was the first time at this particular institution—and I've been here since I think 2012 or 2013—and this was the first semester where I ran into it, and I said, "You know what, you all are confused, and it's really, really sad that we live in a world that I've got to be 'power over' for you to respect your own quality of work."

Linda: Yes. Let's bring it back to race for a minute.

Kalima: Oh, yes, because that was a huge part of it.

Linda: Because being professors of color also is like we're cool.

Kalima: Folks of color and whites across the board.

Mohan: Do you attribute their confusion or whatever that is to how they perceived your race and being a woman and all that?

Kalima: Yes. partly so.

Mohan: That they thought, "Well, she's going to just be …"

Kalima: She's going to be understanding. She's going to be cool or that I don't represent the same manifestations or the same markers of power that they're accustomed to, so they can challenge it in a very specific way and think that it's okay and also think, "Oh, that's not even her politics," but you will respect me. You will respect the process. You will respect me the same way in which I respect you, and I respect this profession.

Linda: Yes. Do they feel like they have to turn in the white professor's paper on time, but they can get an extension from you? There are all of those dynamics, and, oh, we have this connection, so, therefore, you should understand that I'm in the middle of whatever kind of struggle, and so I did the best I could with the paper, right?

Kalima: The thing is they push, for me, they push me into a corner because it really forces me to figure out how am I going to actualize my values. Steve, you used to always say, "How do we concretize our values in action?" and I have to say to myself, "How am I going to do this because I am down for you?" I'm definitely down for you. Majority of you all are women, working-class women, trying to do it out here. I'm down for you, but you will not disrespect this process. You will not disrespect or dishonor the being down because me being down for you is also a risk for me because I'm going against the status quo. You're not respecting what I'm trying to create here.

Mohan: You share this with students?

Kalima: Oh, yes. I had an honest conversation to a point where they …

Mohan: Then how do they respond?

Kalima: The dean had to advise, "stop talking to this person because you are going above and beyond by having this conversation." Students will continuously say, "you didn't tell me that three absences were too many." Or "I didn't know you wouldn't accept a late paper without formal prior approval." They actually have said something wild like that. It was like, "You're in your final year of graduate school. I don't have to tell you that." I am however, going to support you, and I'm going to tell you, you need to make the best decision towards your graduate career and push back to hold them to a high standard.

Steve: It's interesting you raised this because it can feel very isolating like it's being done—some of this is being done—to you because you're a woman of color and because you take the risks you do. I heard implicitly you saying the same thing, Linda. I've also had this experience a lot. I would say it's probably stopped a couple of years ago but only a couple of years ago, probably because I got as old as I am, and maybe they felt, I don't know. They gave up.

Maybe it'll come back soon, but I cannot tell you how people have said to me for years the same thing, not so much about the absences from class but about doing lesser work on papers and thinking because my desire for the shared learning experience was real, that somehow that thing about being equal learners is somehow translated to lesser standards.

Linda: Right.

Steve: I've had so many people, so many students say to me, "I thought you were a nice guy." I've said, "I am a nice guy."

Linda: You were honest.

Steve: It has nothing to do with the dropping of standards.

Kalima: Exactly.

Steve: I think embedded in a lot of people's idea of niceness, it's softness, it's lowered standards, which we in social work by the way, have to struggle with the idea that niceness is a lesser quality.

Kalima: In general.

Steve: We're being empathic, so some think that means we can't be tough in the sense of holding to a standard and holding to an expectation. Linda, you were speaking the other day about the standard of the NASW awards dinner. Was it maybe a high standard that some in the field have dropped? That's true in the ...

Mohan: In the classroom.

Steve: ... in the classroom, too, that being warm and supportive is not about lesser standards. I know I've said this to you. I have two phrases I've learned: "I respect you enough to always challenge you" and then the other is, "You need skills to match your ability." I work a lot on this issue that can sometimes come up, in particular with students of color who have not been provided a set of standards in their undergraduate programs. There also are some white students from working-class backgrounds who've gone to mid-level schools who also haven't been prepared, either, but here in New York City, it has some racial disproportionality woven into this, too. It took me about ten years to come up with that phrase: "You need to get the skills to match your ability." It was so important that the issue of performance be framed correctly. Stating it this way, I saw that a student was smart, and yet he/she/they had been denied skill acquisition, as opposed to "You did a bad paper. This is really poorly written. Your concept is unclear."

If you lead from the critique, all that happens from that is shame, and it intensifies the issues of what people may have experienced in other areas of our lives that we've spoken about in this book. I had a student who had a 4.0 and was the valedictorian of a college that was predominantly all students of color. Her first paper was truly a mess. It had a lot of really good ideas and concepts but had no organization, had run-on sentences, poor grammar, incorrect pronouns.

I went to her; we met, and it turned out she'd been this valedictorian and that she was the number one in her class. She choked up when I spoke with her, and I did, too, because I told her someone's done you a great disservice because you are enormously smart, and you've been cheated from being able to fully demonstrate your intelligence. This is where I learned that phrase. I said, "But you don't have the skills to match." She was clearly a gifted person. She went to the writing center and by the end of the term was close to where she deserved to be. By the time she graduated, she was getting honors. However, she did the work because she had the time and ability to do all that added work—no little kids at home, a flexible job situation. Not every student has those advantages.

Yet even as I say this, I start to get angry again because that story shows up so often, and I still hear faculty say, "I can't believe the crap that this person wrote." As opposed to, "Where did they go to school?" or whatever one says where the teacher pauses to find out if the student got the opportunity to learn the quality training that perhaps you and I got.

Linda:	Yes.
Steve:	Working with this is just another dimension of showing respect without backing off standards to somebody's story. It's all about this idea of being genuine with people, being caring and warm, and also funny in class at times, and it has nothing to do with dropping standards.
Kalima:	Oh, my gosh. That is hitting me so clear, Steve. That is hitting me so in my spirit because I'm living this out in my own personal life where my partner is like mush. Our nieces come in crying, "Kalima won't write my paper for me. I sent her a draft, and she won't edit it." If I edit the paper, I practically have to write it all over again.
Mohan:	Yeah, I feel that way.
Kalima:	Right?
Mohan:	Yeah, people don't remember.
Kalima:	He's like, "Well why do you have such high standards? Why are you so hard on them? Why won't you just do it?" I'm like, "First of all, she's a sophomore in college and writing like this, she has been failed." I told him, "Let me tell you something, when I was working at one of these nonprofits, the executive director got really close with the grantors, and one of the grantors said 'they do not give or they hardly ever give grants out to organizations run by folks of color.'"
	The executive director just flat out asked one of the folks who was on the grant-making committee, what is up with that? She's like, "Folks of color don't know how to write. That's what's up with that. You all just don't know how to write." When she came back and told us that, of

course it was like a freaking microaggression, but it was on some levels a mirror. We all had to look back and say so many of us have been failed in that way. Nobody has ever said to me, "You need to work on your writing."

The one person who said it to me will live in my heart forever. Her name is Dr. Barbara Joseph. She was my field instructor for the Undoing Racism Internship Project (URIP). I wrote a process recording, and she called me on her telephone, and she said something similar to what you said, "you've got to learn how to write."

I just kept writing and writing and writing until I got better at writing, because she told me that. I got through college thinking that I was fine with writing, and it took somebody in graduate school—not in my classrooms, in my field—to be honest with me. The poor writing was probably because I was emoting in my field my process recordings, but that's still no reason to not write properly, you know?

Mohan: No.

Kalima: We need to be having these conversations. Folks need to know and understand just because I'm in a relationship with you that does not mean I'm going to hold you to a lesser standard. In fact, I'm going to heighten my standards because I believe in you that much, and I see the urgency in this work in a way that you can't see it yet.

Linda: Right. I have a question for us as a group then. I suspect that those of us who are of color feel that that issue of standards gets challenged more.

Kalima: Of course.

Linda:	Right? Consciously or unconsciously. Steve you were suggesting you've seen it, so do we just want to leave it as this, which is we've all had this experience or do we really feel like there's something more there?
Steve:	Keep going.
Kalima:	No, there is definitely something …
Mohan:	No, I think there's something big here. I think we're answering like three different questions, which is fine. As I've been listening to this whole thing about standards, I'll say that I haven't experienced that as a person of color.
Kalima:	I didn't think that you would, and I'm going to take … well, you keep going.
Mohan:	So you're not surprised?
Kalima:	I'm not surprised.
Mohan:	Why aren't you surprised?
Kalima:	Because you're South Asian, and with you comes this idea that you are super smart. You are the model minority.
Linda:	You are from the nerdy culture, right. *(Everyone laughs.)*
Steve:	You're probably an Indian with really good math skills.
Kalima:	Yes, you are above and beyond.
Mohan:	Actually, I have an undergraduate in Engineering.
Kalima:	See, he's an engineering social worker. *(More laughter.)*

Mohan: Still that's not fair. He knew already. He knows I have an undergraduate in engineering, so he knows my resume.

Kalima: People see you, and they see high intelligence. They see this person is super smart, and so they attach a value.

Mohan: Even before I say a word.

Kalima: You don't have to say a word, they attach it. You look smart. You dress smart. Did you see him at the NASW-NYC Awards Dinner?

Steve: Oh, yeah, he was fine.

Linda: He looks so good, I know. *(Laughter all around.)*

Kalima: He was so sharp. You come off classy. Your coat last night—I saw you with that coat, and I said, "Good looking Mohan." You come off with an air of what they give you—credibility, legitimacy, respect that you haven't yet even earned, right? In a way, you're not going to be seen as down for people. You're seen as brown, but you're not seen as brown.

Mohan: I know. That's why for the record I've always had a problem with the blanket phrase person of color because I get lumped into that, and you and I have more, Steve, I think you and I have more similar experiences.

Steve: In education.

Mohan: That's why I can relate to you so much because I see a lot of similarities, and when you talk about privilege, I feel like I share a lot of that same privilege with you, and we have totally different skin color. This whole thing about skin color in this country— I've not been questioned in terms of my credibility.

Now, part of that is that I come in knowing my stuff, but a lot of it is unearned also. It's like when you, Linda, talked in one of the really early conversations about walking into the classroom. In fact, I didn't mention you by name, but I told my students about you in my undergraduate class when we were talking about intersectionality. I actually had mentioned, "Oh, I'm working with a colleague on a book, and we're talking about racism."

What you said was so powerful. I had mentioned how when you walk into the room, Linda, and you immediately have to face people scrutinizing you for your credibility.

Linda: Exactly.

Mohan: They were writing a paper about oppression and privilege, areas of their identities where they feel oppressed and privileged. I was sharing about how you and I are working on this book together, and how you and I are both people of color, and how when you walked into the room, you have to face that sense of scrutiny, and that I have never felt that walking into a classroom.

Now, I may feel my own insecurities just because of my insecurities, but I've never felt like people are questioning my credibility because of my color. I wonder whether it's also intersected with gender there. I don't know about that. I wanted to put that out there for the people who are reading this book, who are people of color, but then I think we have to connect skin color with race, with ethnicity, with immigration history.

We have to connect all these. These are all wrapped up. It's not just about skin color. It's about the meanings of the skin color, intersected with all these other things.

Steve: We were connecting this to the issue of standards, of perceived standards, and who is going to be perceived as being able to have those standards.

Mohan: I'm just trying to see how I relate to that whole thing about standards. I think sometimes I question whether I'm too lenient sometimes with standards, but I don't know if it's coming out of a place of this whole idea of community and having process and all that.

I do see—especially with the students I'm teaching right now—I can see the effects of not learning, not developing skills that I've taken for granted. Certain writing skills especially that I've taken for granted, so that's why I often allow revisions.

Linda: Me, too.

Kalima: Of course.

Steve: We need to.

Mohan: I'm like, "That's actually the real world; when you have to write something for publication, you have to revise it." It's kind of the notion that you're going to get it right on the first try?

Steve, when you mentioned colleagues who immediately get angry at students for how they write, there's an implicit statement in that upset about their motivation, that the student wasn't motivated enough to produce a good enough paper. We actually really don't even know that. (See Side Box 13.) I had a student one year who turned in a paper that he thought he worked really hard on, and he got a four out of ten on it. It was devastating for him. He's brand new to this country in our master's program. I remember having a conversation with him. He came

Box 13: How We're Judged by Our Output

As you consider how your own "output" may cause you to be perceived in other people's eyes, consider the following:

- Notice what "conclusions" you make about your students' interest, motivations, and abilities based on their performance on assignments and in class.
- Remember that a student's performance on a task needs to be judged for what it is and nothing more.
- Every performance has a history.
- Remember that there is a person behind every paper.
- Remember that abilities and skills are not the same; we often make unjustified conclusions about a student's abilities based on our assessment of their skills.

up to me at the end of class, and you could tell he was holding back the tears. To be that professor who basically failed him on a paper—brand new immigrant to this country, he had all these hopes. I remember having this conversation with him, and I said, "This is not a reflection on you or what kind of social worker you are. This is about your writing skills." Then he shared with me, he said, "Professor, when I went to my school before nobody's ever asked me to write anything like this."

Steve: There you are.

Mohan: "I never had to share my opinion about things." Then I was like, "Oh, well, then it makes sense, so …" but I could tell he was feeling devastated.

Kalima: Mm-hmm (*affirmative*).

Mohan: Who knows what it means for him to then have to face his own family. It was a ten-point paper, it's not like the end of it, but for him that's my world. I remember it was one of those moments as if it were yesterday, when I was talking with laser sharpness, where how I handled that was going to be crucial. Long story short, I recommended that he contact a person in our department who helps specifically with the writing. I said, "Contact him." He emailed me the next morning, and he said, "Professor, I set up an appointment with this man." Over the course of the year, I saw paper after paper get better and better, but I remember that moment was critical. I felt a part of me was like,

"Oh, I'm the person who's giving him a 40 on a paper," but I have to because that's what he earned on the paper.

Steve: You gave him hope actually because he can improve now, because part of the learning process, I think, is we look back and see what happened afterwards. Again, this only happens with the experience of teaching where we are with students, where we see that this progress is possible. We learned how capable they are, and out of that they gain that stature of authority where we also know that if it doesn't happen, Kalima's point about grants will come into play. I've said this in many classes, "You will get through this program, and you will never be promoted to be a director, and that's shame on me if I don't work with you on that."

Mohan: I didn't understand what you meant by that.

Steve: Everybody wants to have a multiracial workforce, but they're not going to promote somebody to the level where they write grants as directors and ...

Linda: That's right. Suddenly you can't compete.

Steve: ... your executive directors and associate executives. They don't get to that level. Leaders become happy with whoever is out in front working one-on-one with people, but that executiveship is only possible with the skill level and the practice of thinking like that student had never been challenged to think. In the end, deep, reflective thinking becomes a repository of the few. It makes it easy for people to say, "We'd love to have more African Americans and Latinos, but look at the difference, look at the skill level." At that point, there's no time to catch up. You've got to have somebody write the grant. You've got to have somebody who's going to meet with the board. You've got to have somebody who can handle going out to different groups of constituents or whatever it might be. It just doesn't happen.

Kalima: I don't know if this is our collective experience, like when you were saying, "Oh, they said I'm a nice guy." We're in the academy, but I would believe that most of us are probably in a very contentious relationship with the academy, right? We realize that we are there for a reason; we don't like the way the academy operates. We don't like the way in which they represent things sometimes, like how they come out on issues and things of that sort, but we realize that there is a purpose. There's a very clear purpose of why we're in there.

Sometimes having these conversations with students, especially when we're talking about the non-profit industrial complex, and if you give the reading, "Social Service or Social Change," by Paul Kivel.

Mohan: I love that article. Oh, my gosh.

Kalima: It's great. They already know your politics is maybe 56% oppositional to the academy. There becomes this expectation that since you're so radical, you will take grades less seriously and have the same oppositional relationship with the standard. I keep saying, "No, I don't perform my values in this way." I was with a colleague the other day who is way more radical in the expression of their politics than I am, so they'll throw F-bombs all over the place and don't give a rat's ass about it. I'm uncomfortable with that because I'm sort of imagining my own respectability politics in that space. Then I remind myself that on some levels, students like the performance of radicalism. They want you to be performing radicalism like dismissing standards of excellence and using particular language in the classroom, when the

> **Performing Radicalism:** *nominally challenging the status quo by defining standards of excellence as tools of the oppressor, using particular language in the classroom as a marker of not being part of the system, and/or outright disregarding the function of an educational institution to nurture concrete skills (like writing) as a demonstration of radicalism.*

radical freaking thing to do is to hold you to your highest possibility …

Linda: Yes, thank you.

Kalima: … because you were never ever meant to get this far anyway.

Steve: That's right.

Kalima: That is what boggles me. You like this performance of cursing out the academy, and this is about the academy, blah, blah, blah the academy, while this very same person is fighting to stay in the academy because the academy gives this person, or these folks, legitimacy in their own personal lives. This behavior also, for some students, equates to us saying basically fuck the standards of the academy, and let's do something different. No, no, no, honey. Do you understand that I need you to go out into the world and be fully equipped to shake this ship and then to build your leadership?

That's what I need you to do. This is not about the academy; this is me believing in you or what my mandate is to you, what my love is for you, and this profession, and the world that we hold in our hands, and the clients we hold in our hands. This has nothing to do with the academy. I don't give a shit about that, but when you walk out of my classroom, and you got an "A," you worked your ass off to get that A, and nobody can fuck with you because you did your work, and you earned that "A."

Mohan: Amen.

Kalima: Yes, the premise of radicalism to me is like, "Wait, I don't have time for that." My radicalism is my radical love for you, our ancestors, and the world that's ahead of us; that's it. I think that's what happens when folks of color, like they want us to say, "Fuck the system and that." We say it all the time, but not when it comes to you being your best self, no.

Linda: My answer to that is I want them to be bilingual and bicultural, like I am. I could sit and throw the F-bombs like anybody else.

Steve: Yes, you can. (*Everybody laughs.*)

Linda: I can be quite bawdy but I also can—and I want to make sure I'm as fluent as anybody else in the academy— speak whatever I need to speak, and have the wisdom to know the difference.

Steve: That's good. I think the ability to fully love others requires us to be able to love ourselves with who we are. Obviously, for the four us in this little conversation, each of us has a different story.

It's all about arriving at a level of self-love to be both present to our authority without turning it into that God-awful stuff that we experienced in other parts of our lives, being abused in one way or another. It means that that authority is not going to be used to dominate somebody else; it's going to be used to help people see that they, too, can have the same kind of authority, that they, too, can rise and meet expectations that they never knew they could.

As you said, Kalima, I'm a real believer in Freire, too. I try to live by what Freire talks about when he says the stuff about only the oppressed can free the oppressor and themselves from our mutual dehumanization. I really believe that in the sense that as I'm able to claim my authority and love, I'm able to see how much other people are giving me, which frees me to be more relaxed and less worried about power as belonging to me. I'm not into that thing anymore, although I could play it if I have to, but as you said, Linda, that ability to be in this "to be fully human is to be incomplete" also means that we could be silly. We could be funny. We could be down-to-earth. We could be gentle, *and* we're not backing off standards. It's not about "less than." It's not about—oh, therefore, because you've been oppressed, things like standards don't matter that much more.

Linda: Exactly.

Steve: It's interesting, I think in this guide's conversations we're finding one of the big issues is our ability to hold authority in different ways. We have ended up talking about developing the ability to create a different learning environment that has teaching and learning and content and process integrated in new and powerful ways. Well, actually they're not new, but they're being reimagined and recreated in our conversations.

The secret is there is no secret, but it's what we're finding inside ourselves to make us able to do some of this work about working with people perceived as different from us, or the fact we're able to see how much we share and how much we care. As you were saying, Kalima, acknowledging the very differences that exist that have given me a very advantaged life and then using them in ways that allow others to experience opportunities inside the classroom that maybe they haven't had elsewhere, admitting that such a classroom takes struggle to create, both for each of us and for the students, with everyone able to feel self-respect and their own humanity.

Mohan, Kalima, Linda: Yes!

Guiding Principles and Strategies

Assessment and grading elicits many emotions, ethical considerations, and challenges for all parties involved. It is not a value-free process, nor can it be stripped of its vulnerability to impact the way identity impacts the assessment from beginning to end.

- Principle: It is important for faculty to clearly delineate deal breakers in their pursuit of being anti-racism practitioners. This demands a strict inventory of values and expectations, which should be communicated to students as early as possible.
- Strategy: The act of crystallizing expectations at the onset of the relationship sets up a space of truth and clarity that can be referenced in the chance of disagreement. An authentic relationship is based entirely on truth and clear boundaries. It is up to faculty to be clear, yet allow enough space for adults to make self-determining decisions.
- Principle: Authentic relationships with students are a tool for effective teaching/facilitating and learning. Being in relationship with students or participants never replaces the primary reason why the teacher/facilitator and student have been brought together. For some students, power sharing in the classroom is unfamiliar and difficult to navigate.
- Strategy: Faculty/facilitators must pay close attention to the way their relationships with students are playing out. At the slightest onset of tension, critically and empathically engage. Use what happened as a way to identify underlying assumptions and deepen the learning process.

Each of us walks into the classroom and must face questions about our legitimacy. Some of us gain credibility by not doing a thing because of who we are perceived to be. Some of us are denied credibility by not doing a thing simply because of who we are perceived to be.

- Principle: Our identities have been shaped by our lived experience, and our lived experience has, in turn, been shaped by our identities. Our students may ask us directly or indirectly, "Who are you in your identities to be teaching me in my identities?"
- Strategy: Expect students to question your legitimacy and credibility and see this questioning process as an invitation to authentically engage with one another's identities.

In cultivating community with our students, we also have the authority and responsibility to assess. This duality can create tension for both instructors and students. Following on Parker Palmer's ideas about "creative tension," we can work with this tension as a necessary paradox in building relationships within the crucible of power. Building community with our students does not mean we sacrifice standards. In fact, it demands a laser focus on standards in the service of our profession and practice. Interrogate your own relationship to having authority in order to claim it in a powerful and loving way.

- Principle: If one is committed to anti-racism and anti-oppression work as part of the classroom experience, both in terms of content and in examining how it is lived, a faculty member must be willing to address her/his/their own issues related to power and authority and whether or not one implicitly plays a "zero-sum" game with students.
- Strategy: Be willing to examine issues of power, privilege, and positionality inside the classroom itself and not just in larger social forces. Work on your own comfort with your authority related to knowledge-building, grading, and openness to learning from those with less power—students. Recognize that this examination and exploration is a lifelong commitment and requires a willingness to struggle openly with other faculty and students throughout your career.

At different moments, each of us are both student and teacher. Regardless of our position and role, each of us wants to feel valued and to know that we have something to offer. We need to consider: What makes "facilitating" different from "teaching"? In so doing, we need to reflect on what we consider "content" and what we consider "process."

- Principle: Value students for what they can teach, and see teaching as an integral part of learning.
- Principle: Find ways to challenge the (false) dichotomy between content and process. There is a process in content and content in process.
- Strategy: Create assignments and activities that genuinely convey the message to students that what they have to teach is valued, unique, and necessary.

CONVERSATION SEVENTEEN

Question: *How do we encourage this work inside and outside the classroom, yet include self-care that pays attention to trauma, stress and pain, and the health of our bodies, especially as it is activated in faculty of color?*

Background to this conversation:
The recurring awareness of the degree of pain and revisited trauma on the part of so many faculty of color as these topics unfolded made clear that issues of self-care were not a luxury but a necessity. At the same time, there was an equal insight that attending to self-care, given so many other demands, is often challenging.

Observations and Reflections:
The importance of well-being, whether for those in child welfare, homelessness, or education, has been well-established. While we educators often espouse this value, how often do we accomplish the balance between work and life that allows for self-care as an integrated part of our lives?

> **Self-Care:**
> *Self-care is a set of attitudes and practices to nurture one's being physically, emotionally, spiritually, socially, and psychologically. Teachers, social workers, and other helping professionals come into the field and are trained to focus on helping others; self-care is about prioritizing one's own well-being, which in turn will enhance one's ability to be present and available for others.*

THE CONVERSATION

Steve: Maybe this will be a shorter conversation! *How do we encourage this work inside and outside the classroom, yet include self-care that pays attention to trauma, stress and pain, and the health of our bodies, especially if it is activated in faculty of color?*

Mohan: You were just talking earlier about that, the body ...

Kalima: That's my question. Earlier, I talked about folks who I look at, like some white folks, and I'm like, "Wow, what does it mean to be so light?" They're just so happy all the time or seemingly happy and just laughing, and ...

Steve: Seemingly.

Linda: Seemingly.

Kalima: They don't have folks being killed in the streets every other week. What does it mean to live in that existence? When I get to that space, I realize like, "Oh, you need to take some kind of break from the work because that means your joy filter is pretty low at this point." What I have always done, and I've told people to do, is always to create a community of love, and resistance so that you have fun together, and you do the critical organizing or the critical thinking work together and be committed to that. I love Emma Goldman. One of the things she said in her book *Living My Life* is that she doesn't want to be a part of a revolution that doesn't dance or that doesn't party, right?

Mohan: Right.

Kalima: That was a hard life, but she knew how to have fun as well, and she enjoyed herself like so many of us. I think about the black church. The people would be organizing and then go to the black church and sing and dance and clap and eat. I always think about the ways in which they took care of their souls in this work and in one another as ways to be a real organizer or to be really committed to this work. Commitment doesn't mean that you always have to be immersed in it and always talking about it or always sad or angry about it.

Mohan: So true.

Kalima: You can have fun, right? We need to diversify our images of a real organizer and even begin to dissect this idea there is such a thing as a real organizer. What's real activism? Once we've done that, then figure out who do you get to be in the work? We get to have fun. Having fun and doing this work is very, very necessary because the thrust of it is unending. Not only seeing it, experiencing it, you've got to read about it, you watch movies about it, you've got to have conversations about it all the while working to end it. That all is stuff that we're carrying. We need a place to let it go and to take care of ourselves. Having spaces of communities—I call it community of love and resistance—I didn't make it myself, bell hooks made it up, and you can see that bell hooks is my favorite person in the world. James Baldwin is second.

I need to bring more of Baldwin's *The Fire Next Time* because that's a really good book. We must intentionally and forcefully create those types of spaces, and the other thing is, to find your tribe as well as our our creative outlets in this work, too. It's not a deep response, but because it lives so deeply in me, I need it to be simple.

Steve: Oh, I disagree. I thought that was very, very deep.

Kalima: Oh, my God.

Mohan: It was also practical, right? Things we can actually do. It's interesting this question came out. I felt the need to do some yoga poses because of the intensity of our conversation. *(Does a yoga exercise in the group.)* No, this is a good hip opener because that's actually where we hold all of the pain, emotional pain. I guess having been somebody who ignored my body for the first part—half of my life—I was all head. One big huge analytical …

Steve: Engineer.

Mohan: I do tell my students about paying attention to the body. Ten, 15 years ago, I probably would never have said that, but it's because of where I'm at in my life, and realizing that without the body, none of that really matters, right? There's no point.

Bring in all kinds of practices with the body. Try to be as aware of the body as possible, exercising, moving, eating lunch. I tell my students, "Please do not skip your lunch. Please do not sit at your desk and eat lunch, even in your field work internships. You have an hour lunch for a reason. You go, leave the desk. Don't sit there with your lunch."

But I think also we've been socialized to think we're not supposed to do that. I'm like, that's really, really unhealthy. Going to the whole thing about humor, I love what you said about laughing. Again, I'm going to reference meditation, but one of the greatest meditation teachers that's out there is Pema Chödrön. She says in one of her teachings that if we meditate without a sense of humor, we look like we've sucked on 100 lemons, something like that. I'm paraphrasing, but she basically says, if you don't have a sense of humor about this, first of all, the meditation is not really going to help you. She constantly says that you have to laugh. You have to watch yourself and be like, there I go again, or there it is again. It's actually taking it very seriously, but it's actually about letting it go, like, "I don't have to." I think that's an important thing, and you need the community of support.

I do tell my students often that we don't do anything alone. We're interdependent from the moment we are created in the womb.

Kalima: The way to live.

Mohan: We're never independent. I don't know what that means, independent, because we're always in relation to somebody, but we forget it. That's what I have to say right now.

Linda: I just feel like self-care is so not my forte. I'm like, "I have no credibility." I preach it, and I remember very vividly preaching it in the organization that I lead, but it didn't matter because people watched what I did, and they saw me not respect boundaries of time, and not go out to lunch, so it didn't matter that I was telling them to do it if I didn't do it. The message they got was, "Kill your damn self, too, because that's what hard work looks like," and that's what I would value. I always feel like this is a tough one. I go, "What can I possible say about that?" It is important to try to communicate that message, and it's important to try to walk it as well.

Mohan: Maybe what would be helpful to the readers, because I bet a lot of people reading the book can relate to what you just said, is to talk about that struggle.

Linda: Mm-hmm *(affirmative)*.

Mohan: That they are right there and could relate.

Linda: Absolutely.

Mohan: There's a point in my life where I was right in your place. In my twenties, I used to pride myself of only needing three hours of sleep. That I could work 18 hours a day. I used to say with great pride, that I could get up at 4:00 in the morning. I used to get up at 4:00 in the morning when I was a high school teacher and then go to work, teach, coach cross country, come home, eat dinner, and work for three more hours, and go to bed at 1:00 in the morning. I did that for four, five years, and then I went to the hospital with a possible heart attack.

I didn't have a heart attack, but it felt like a heart attack. Maybe you could say, what do you think drives you into making it hard for the self-care?

Linda: Right.

Mohan: Because I bet a lot of readers would relate to that.

Linda: Yeah, I mean just that it's not important, that working is more important. It just doesn't come close to being as important as working. There is, I think also a superiority that comes with that. I'm so committed. I do whatever it takes.

Mohan: Look at me.

Linda: Look at me. I am strong, whatever it takes. It's in part cultural also, which we talked about a little bit I think in one of the first sessions, about what it meant to, as a Puerto Rican, you have to show that you are not the stereotype that people think. We are not lazy. We are not dirty. I will work my fingers to the bone. I will work my fingers to the bone even if I am the boss. I will never act entitled, and big, and bigger than you. I'll be right out there with the mop. In fact, I'll still have the mop when you've gone home. Even if you're the janitor, I'll still be there with the mop. There's a superiority that I think is part of it. Yes, it's complicated, so it is wrapped up in some identity issues as well.

Steve: The safety of always being the best and the hardest worker.

Linda: Right.

Steve: No one can accuse you of anything.

Linda: Right. To me, it is the polar opposite of everything negative I associate with being white. It is the complete opposite of being entitled. It's the complete opposite of embracing power, privilege. It says unprivileged, like I'm …

Kalima: Mm-hmm (*affirmative*).

Mohan: It's almost like you have to be the extreme opposite.

Linda: Yes.

Steve: That is really deep.

Mohan: Definitely.

Kalima: Mm-hmm (*affirmative*). On both ends because on one end you'll find an identity of being lazy; on the other, you'll find the identity of being entitled.

Linda: Exactly.

Kalima: You have not found your own space.

Linda: You can imagine, therefore, how exhausting that is, and that there's no freaking choice. It's like, I've got to write you my therapy check. Seriously. No, because I realized that that is so important.

Mohan: We talked about the loss of identity in the 2016 Presidential Election question, what we may lose from the shared commonality in emphasizing social difference. There's a loss here, too, right? I mean, for you to not work hard that way, all the time. Like you were talking about identity ...

Linda: The structures.

Mohan: ... the structure of our society ...

Kalima: As capitalistic ...

Mohan: ... and also being a Puerto Rican.

Linda: I've got to be twice as good, three times as good.

Mohan: Yeah, and that's real.

Linda: That is real.

Mohan: That's not made up. That's not made up at all.

Kalima: I was recently reading about the "mammification" of black women—something by bell hooks, I think.

Steve: You read all the light stuff. *(Group laughter.)*

Kalima: I thought this was going to be light, and I'm like deep in it with this book by Shonda Rhimes, *Year of Yes*. I mean I laugh all the time, but she's talking about some real stuff.

I wrote a paper critiquing one of her characters, Bailey, on the TV show *Grey's Anatomy*. I wrote, "She's just a mammy at this point." I just went in on it, but it is the mammification of black women in positions of power, where we feel a sense of responsibility to develop and to take care of and to be opposite from what we have seen in society, so we spend extra time in these roles, and doing these caretaking positions. You don't ever want to feel like you're better than the janitor because you know we all know where we come from, and we know …

Linda: Yeah, and I know people will look at me and think, "Is she the janitor?"

Kalima: Exactly. We know that part of our role is to be in solidarity with that janitor because we want to care for them. It's the mammification. How do we live the "both and" of this? We do want to be in solidarity, we do want to develop. We want to be here to have these critical conversations with white folks and people of color and bring them along and stuff like that, but also that part of what we never got to do and our ancestors never got to do is care, radically care for ourselves. Self-care doesn't have to be self, it can be community care.

What does that actually look like? One of the things that I've learned to do is to bring games into the classrooms. Let's just get silly or let's play this game. We play speed dating. We play a game where I place a word on your forehead, and people have to give you clues, and you have to try to guess what's on your forehead.

Mohan: Oh, I know that. That's a great game.

Kalima: All this stuff. We start off with a whole bunch of games and laughter. I bring in wild podcasts that will have you cracking up. Doing the work but also infusing joy and that works because it's part of our care, if we're going to be committed to doing it.

Linda: Mm-hmm *(affirmative)*.

Kalima: The mammification is real, and that sounds like what you're doing.

mammification: *derived from the historically based caricature of "mammy," mammification is the process of women of color becoming default caretakers of folks in anti-racism movements or organizations. Rather than assuming a leadership role in terms of direction and strategy, women of color, particular black women, assume and are expected to care for and make everything right for others while ignoring themselves and their own direct responsibilities.*

Linda: Yeah, and I don't want to lose the solidarity with the people who are in the struggle, who are also my family, literally my family members. I am the first generation to get that degree. I do not want to lose my solidarity with them, and I don't want to forget from where I came, my identity.

Kalima: Yeah, so you pick up a broom now and again.

Linda: I impose on myself, I impose this on myself to make sure that I don't forget, will not take the risk and forget it. One of my memories I'll never forget it. It was at the Administration for Children's Services, and one of my supervisees said to me, "You act like you're just the girl behind the desk, not the associate commissioner, just the girl behind it." You know, I just happen to be behind the desk, but I'm not a big shot.

Mohan: I'm just thinking a similar thing happens for me, but it comes from wanting to disown my privilege. I've talked in other questions about my struggles around my own class privilege and caste privilege, and all that stuff. There's a part of me that when at work, when our administrative assistant makes copies for me, I always feel guilty.

Kalima: What? For her doing the job that you paid her to do?

Mohan: I don't feel like it's right for her to make my copies. I should have to do my own. I grew up believing that if I've dirtied my dish, I wash my dish. Nobody should have to wash my dishes, but it's not coming from a place of trying to compensate for what society might assume about me. It's actually coming from a place of like, "Eww, I don't want to be that." To really own my status or privilege is like ...

Linda: I get that. I don't want to be the entitled prick who makes somebody …

Mohan: No, so I want to be known as the person that … Like, I make friends with the cleaning people. It's not because I'm trying to prove anything. There's also a piece of me though that doesn't want to be this the guy with the Ph.D. that's just having somebody make copies for him. I believe that I should do that. That's not somebody else's job, to take care of me like that. I'm just putting that in there because it's similar, but it's coming from a different place.

Steve: It's interesting. We've talked earlier about becoming comfortable in authority in the classroom that we're not going to abuse our authority in the classroom. We attempt to hold our authority without creating domination. This is just a variation of that discussion, only outside of the classroom. Whether it's we don't want the janitor to feel that we think we're better than him or be perceived as having risen above, even though in society, the "risen above" is structurally true. You're making four times as much as the janitor. You do have to have a Ph.D., blah, blah, blah.

There is a structural dimension in these positions that's real, and learning to distinguish the difference between being comfortable with and being bothered by the structural differences that exist—that's got a lot of unfairness and inequity built into it. At the same time, being okay with who we are is another part of that struggle because the logic of this argument, unless we were to have this amazing overthrow of these kinds of structural conditions, is that secretary will be out of a job, and the janitor will be out of a job, too, and everybody will be a janitor.

Linda: Yeah, how about that?

Steve: I don't think that will work.

Mohan: It won't.

Steve: I know that nobody here is going to be abusing the janitor or the administrative assistant or the custodian. Nobody is going to say, "Hey, you, clean this up. Do my papers." Yet, it just speaks to what we have to struggle with, both in the classroom and out, which is the "fullness of our own humanity that's always incomplete," my old phrase from Paulo Freire. It's just amazing, and part of this guide is we're modeling for people, for the readership, that, yes, we have all done some things right, and hopefully some are helpful.

At the same time, part of our message that we have to give to whoever is reading this is we're also always in struggle. (See Side Box 14.) There's nobody here who feels finished, done, and we've got the answer. The self-care stuff, the work on this is forever and ever. I've arrived at a point as I've told you, I've never had social oppression in my life until I arrived at being perceived as old. Structurally, I am old. In terms of lifespan, I call it late autumn.

For the first time in my life, I begin to experience things like, Where do my wife and I get placed at a table when we go into a restaurant? Restaurant managers don't want to sit us in the middle as much because that's where the action is. It may be that they had four reservations, and there was no room, but I'm asking myself, "Am I over here because I'm old?" For the first time, I've begun to have to struggle again about something big. I feel vulnerable about a dimension of my social identity that all of you have lived with all your lives in other ways.

Now, lo and behold, in my self-care, part of my commitment as to why I continue to work out has always been to deal with my anger and my upset about the way the world is. Now, some of it is, "Goddamn it, I'm not going to let people perceive me as some doddering old fool." I've got another layer of what I now struggle with that I never had to struggle with before. Like with all these questions, the question about self-care is a lifetime thing, always changing.

It's this claiming who we are that is always open to reconfiguration. It speaks to another point people made, that we need each other. We need to be with people who we trust, and they trust us. We can be vulnerable and have a struggle and not have it used against us because otherwise if we only keep it in our own heads, we can't do the kind of examination and that growth. We need each other.

Kalima, Linda, Mohan: Amen!

Box 14: What It Means to Be "In Struggle"

There are two kinds of struggle: 1) external, where you act on your beliefs in some form or fashion to combat racism, sexism, and other forms of oppression, and 2) internal struggle, where you make the *internal effort*, where one mindfully reflects on and tests assumptions about how the world is and our place within it. Examples include:

- Joining in actions, whether petitions or demonstrations, that actively support our beliefs and work to define those under attack from further injustice;
- Raising (at faculty meetings and other smaller settings) issues of implicit and/or explicit bias that may occur.

Guiding Principles and Strategies

While self-care is a core principle and value in social work, the practice of it is scarcely realized by many professionals in the field. Due to many implicit and explicit barriers, social work professionals, particularly some of those belonging to systemically marginalized identities, find it hard to actually engage in meaningful care or to even be cared for within community.

- Principle: For faculty and folks involved in anti-racism work, self-care must not be seen or regarded as a catchy or even sexy phrase we bestow on students or employees with urgency, yet dismiss ourselves. It has to be a core practice and value in our everyday lives.
- Strategy: Faculty should be supported in thinking about and developing creative ways to bring an element of self-care into their classrooms. This can be done by incorporating games such as icebreakers, intentional time to stretch and drink water, and/or something as simple as coloring during scheduled breaks.
- Principle: For faculty of color and who have systemically marginalized identities, self-care is most often a more present need given the daily assaults they must contend with. Particular attention must be paid to this cohort.
- Strategy: Prioritize check-ins, supervision, a self-care plan, and built-in time to commune during the work day. The work of self-care should not fall entirely on the professional; there are way more incentives in the workplace to ignore the self than there are to be mindful of care. Instead, organizations and institutions should commit to an explicit self-care plan and, if possible, benefit package.
- Principle: Folks with troubled histories around worth as it relates to production, value as it relates to their bodies, and class status, need a space to explore these less obvious challenges to self-care.
- Strategy: Include self-care in the supervision process. Implement trauma-informed practices throughout the agency, and continuously recognize the ways societal incidents of violence, degradation, and invisibility impact folks differently. Allot an annual amount of time for staff to leave at a moment's notice in response to a traumatic (racially or otherwise) event.

A SPECIAL CONVERSATION: EIGHTEEN

Question: *How did each of us come to do this work?*

Elizabeth (cover artist): I am so happy to be a part of this book as both an artist and social worker. Often times artists are seen as accessories to the movement work. We are here to beautify a space, but not ourselves seen a cultural community organizers. As social workers, we are seen only as clinicians who work within systems, and not as system changers. Both of these stereotypes do not represent the fierce power that artists and social workers are capable of, all while moving in a ethic of love.

Often times in social justice spaces words like alllyship become an intellectual conversation rather then a transformational connection. In this painting the two people are looking at each other as they pull back the curtain of oppression to work towards humanity. This movement is rooted in love and justice, which allows for growth. Ultimately, our social justice sunsets that we strive for are not rooted in the organizations that we work for, but rather in our willingness to engage in "the work" with each other. The two people in the painting are in commitment to each other.

For me, this art piece on the guide's cover represents the overlap of art, social justice, and healing that shows what world is possible if we choose to create it. I am so pleased to be part of a book that seeks that same possibility! (Elizabeth's art may be seen at www. elizabethrossiart.com)

Kalima: When asked, "How did you come to do this work?" I answer, "The work came to me." As a deeply melaninated Afro-Latina woman with decisively African features, the work of anti-racism came to me as soon as I entered the world. I simply accepted the invitation. My mom said that when I was around three years old, I told her that my grandma did not like me because I was "dark skinned." While it took me many years to acquire the language necessary to fully understand my experience, I have always known what I felt and that was a pervasive message of "wrongness" because I was dark skinned. Thanks to *Jet, Ebony,* and *Essence,* prioritized print media in my household, I never internalized that message. In fact, I rejoiced and embraced my blackness.

I consider myself to have spent my lifetime in this work because to love oneself in the skin I'm in is a small revolution. However, my formal entry was during my service with the United States Army. As a paralegal, I saw the horrors of a system and culture that seemingly set men of color and poor white men up for inevitable failure. Again, without the sophisticated language available to me now, I did not know how to talk about what I was seeing. However, I knew what I felt: injustice. Another small revolution began, one that prompted my decision to leave the service.

A number of small revolutions led me to Silberman School of Social Work, which led me to the Undoing Racism Internship Project of the People's Institute for Survival and Beyond where I learned the language, deepened my relationship with self, sharpened my analysis, gained community, and confirmed that

I had arrived at my life's work: anti-racism social work practice and undoing racism.

I have always done this work—it's how I have not just thrived, but survived. Today, it's just in a more formal, public format.

Linda: So, here we are in 2017, looking at this book in which Steve, Kalima, Mohan, and I all revealed so much of ourselves in the quest for understanding, the quest for the shedding of the many "costumes" we wear every day, embodying the many roles we play. What we want is to be seen, to be known, to be understood and appreciated simply for that. It is as elusive as it is simple. So, how is it that today, in 2017, I'm a part of a team that includes a former professor and forever mentor? That I've become a professor like this professor I have looked up to? How did this Puerto Rican kid from Brooklyn come to this particular table?

First and foremost, I'm filled with gratitude as I know that most of the "tables" I have had the privilege to come to have been blessings and that it is completely plausible that I could have never gotten here—gift from my God, no doubt. From my earliest days as a child, issues of race were the soundtrack and wallpaper of my growing up. Like soundtracks and wallpaper, we're not always conscious of them. They're just there in the background. But they gave texture and flavor to the experiences of my life, and issues of race permeated everything from my sense of self-worth, my identity, my aspirations and my ability to trust. It also fueled my passion, my love for others, my commitment to justice. In short, it is part of the DNA that makes me, well, me. The process of working on this book revealed that with great clarity to me.

I was a somewhat pale, olive-skinned Puerto Rican girl with African features such as full lips, a wider nose, and coarse, curly hair when in its natural state. My Puerto Rican father was a white-skinned man with straight, thin hair whose mother was a dark brown-skinned woman with tightly coiled coarse hair and a wide nose and full lips. My Puerto Rican mother is an olive-skinned woman with a narrower nose and thinner lips and straighter hair. Her mother was darker and had coarser hair than she did, but not as coarse as mine. Her father was white-skinned and straight-haired. My little brother was darker than me with silky, curly hair, often described as "Puerto Rican" hair, and his complexion was described as "Indio" or Indian colored. Without anyone having to show me a chart, I came to understand very early on (before age five) which were the character-istics that were more valued and attractive (lighter skin, straighter hair, narrower nose, smaller lips) and which were less desirable. I knew where I stood in the typol-ogy, and no matter how unfair it seemed to me, there was nothing I could do to change it. My mother worked hard to "address" these shortcomings, getting my hair permed, encouraging me not to pout so as not to "allow" my lips to get larger. I somehow knew I'd never success-fully compete in the beauty department. No one who looked like me could be found on TV or in magazines or books. I'd have to distinguish myself in some other way. I wasn't sure where I fit in or belonged. I had black features, but my family didn't consider Puerto Ricans to be black, and I wasn't "black" enough to be embraced by blacks. I wasn't Puerto Rican-looking like the standard of beauty associated with it (long, dark, silky, wavy hair), and I sure wasn't white, despite my light skin.

My cousins teased me for being a "Brillo-head" (mean-ing my hair felt like a Brillo steel wool pad) and for having pork-chop lips. I just wanted to be pretty with long straight hair in pony tails or two long braids. I found my affirmation in school, where learning stimulated me and where my intelligence was appreciated and rewarded. I wasn't pretty and would never be, but I was smart, and I loved school because I was affirmed there. School was my haven, where I found what I loved—learning, reading, writing, math, being competent and good at something. It was a place I could belong, at least intellectually. These experiences have made me attuned to what it feels like to not belong and how much we all want that. Now, I fight for how much we all deserve that, just because we are human. I want to contribute to understanding, to human beings being valued simply because they are human.

I have enormous confidence in the strength of the human spirit to overcome the smallness and pettiness that we can also exhibit as people. I want to contribute to creating opportunities, great and small, where that can happen. This project has been a gift, an opportunity to build strength from vulnerability, hope from fear, commonality from difference, acceptance from rejection. We are building a bridge between these polarities within and between us. These polarities make us human. We have the opportunity to manage these polarities in a way that can also make us humane.

Mohan: When I was first asked if I would like to be a co-author on this guide, it took me all of a half second to decide. Of course I would! Having the opportunity to work on this book comes at a wonderful time in my life. After many years of hiding from myself and hiding from others, I feel like I can be who I am and feel good about who I am. That doesn't mean I don't have moments or even days of self-doubt or want to crawl into a shell, but I feel like I can embrace who I am as an Indian, a person with brown skin, a gay man, an immigrant, a teacher. It wasn't always like this for me. I spent much of my childhood feeling a confusing mix of pride and comfort in my heritage and also a pervasive sense of shame and embarrassment about not belonging or always trying to belong. Much of this had to do with being a brown-skinned Hindu Indian in an almost entirely white Protestant small town in Pennsylvania. Little did I know then that my awkwardness also had to do with feeling different because of my sexuality. One of the great gifts my parents gave me was a sense of history and connection to my homeland, India, and to my large extended multigenerational family. a source of strength and support and groundedness to this day. It has been and still is a struggle to love myself for all of who I am, a struggle I am grateful for, as painful as it can be. Today, I enjoy living each day with my life partner and feel blessed with beautiful friends, families, teachers, students, mentors, and colleagues.

In that spirit of relationships, what a joy it has been to be able to work with my former professor, mentor, colleague, and friend Steve Burghardt and to get to know and collaborate with Linda and Kalima, two inspiring social work educators. To me, this book is first and foremost about the power, beauty, and love of teaching and the preciousness of the relationships we build in the classroom and the field. Writing this book at this moment is all the more special as this is my 25th year as a teacher. Each semester I feel gratitude for having found my calling as a teacher at a young age and to be able to share this excitement with three passionate social workers and educators is a true blessing.

I am grateful for the teachings and practices of meditation, which remind me daily of the gentle power of mindfulness and compassion. To me, this book is also about the daily struggles we all face to have compassion for ourselves and for others. In the course of writing this book, Donald Trump was elected as the 45th President of the United States. This happened amidst a social and political climate that reveals entrenched and pervasive racism, sexism, homophobia, and xenophobia in our country, forces that can be dismantled only through genuine dialogue, for through dialogue we realize our innate and ever-present potential to embrace one another's humanity. As social workers and educators, we have a crucial role to play, and I am happy to be part of it!

Steve: There's nothing like growing up in a community as a happy-go-lucky white kid who went anywhere in a small New England town, did anything, got approval for just walking through the door, and then went home to be afraid. Being chosen to be the star in his kindergarten school play and then terrified over his father's disapproval at his selection creates a very watchful mindset in a boy. Throw in the unearned luck of being born a fraternal twin alongside a beloved sister denied the same opportunities as me, and you develop a pinpoint, albeit jagged, focus on fairness and power—or the lack thereof—as a foundation to my life's work. Frankly, it was pretty easy for me to fight against racial oppression or abusive authority—I had a lived experience that white patriarchs weren't worth much and that opportunity applied to one didn't mean a lot if it wasn't applied to all.

Unfortunately, the jaggedness was as sharp as the insight: As a young man, I detested all authority, only to learn later that I was afraid of my own. Like a lot of humorous people, I could as easily get angry toward people I loved as tell a joke, only able to quell the inner flames as I came to see that so much of that anger was directed at myself. It was painful to realize that being politically correct was much easier than being personally tolerant.

While it would be a stretch to say that Paulo Freire's *Pedagogy of the Oppressed* saved me, there is little question that over many years, it has served as my foundational guide to understand how I have sought to live and act on the world. His words (and, of course, so many others, many referred to throughout this guide), a lot of therapy, loving, bracing family and friends, and the necessity of doing social justice work have healed and sustained me in ways that allow me now to embrace with relief both my fullness as a human being and my incompletion, too.

And thus this guide. It happened almost accidentally, after having one of many rich conversations with Kassie Graves, our publisher. Well before the election of 2016, through our friendship we discussed how difficult it was to have sustained, thoughtful conversations on race, racism, sexism, sexuality and the like inside classrooms and agencies. We both remarked from our different vantage points that a lot of this difficulty had more to do with consternation over what to say and less about active resistance from faculty and students. If people could see a way forward, we agreed, they'd do it.

And so the *Guide* was born. Having had the good fortune of having taught and learned from thousands of remarkable students over the years, I had a wealth of options. That said, asking Kalima, Linda, and Mohan was easy. Obviously, there was to be a social mix, for the same questions lead to different answers based on one's own background and how others react to it. I also knew that these three people were committed to the work of handling issues of race, power, and oppression inside the classroom and out, and that they were conversant on these issues where together we could draw out lessons and insights that might prove helpful to others. Finally, they each had another, subtler quality: They were modest about who they were personally and, while obviously successful, were not driven by professional status.

Of course, what has been revealed through these conversations is something far more powerful than I could have expected. The more we talked about the mechanics of classroom management to handle these conversations, the more our group emphasized the necessity of embracing our own stories—the pain in them, the hurt that lives on in small acts replicated in classrooms and on the street, and then, the miracle of moving past that and using the work on one's self and in the classroom to heal and transform what on paper could have been a life of sorrow but is instead lives of daily, transformative hope and possibility.

As a white man whose lineage includes both the founder of the Pilgrims and the slave owner of W.E. Burghardt Du Bois's grandfather, I am keenly aware that I have not suffered in ways my guide partners have. That I was able to bear witness to all that was revealed here has further enriched my life. Once again, Freire's lesson is squared: only the oppressed can free us all from our mutual dehumanization—including me. Kind reader, may this guide in part serve that possibility for you.

REFERENCES

Blakely, K. (2007). Reflections on the role of emotion in feminist research. *International Journal of Qualitative Methods, 6(2)*, 2–7.

Brown, B. (2012). *Daring greatly: How the courage to be vulnerable transforms the way we live, love, parent, and lead.* New York, NY: Gotham Books.

Burghardt, S. (2016). *Holistic Engagement: Transformative Social Work Education in the 21st Century* . Ed. L. Pyles. New York: Oxford University Press.

Chodron, P. (2002). *The places that scare you: A guide to fearlessness in difficult times.* Boston, MA: Shambhala Publications.

Freire, P. (1995). *Letters to Christina: Reflections on my life and work.* Trans. Donaldo Macedo. New York: Routledge.

— (1995) *Pedagogy of hope: Reviving pedagogy of the oppressed.* Trans. Robert R. Barr. New York: Continuum.

— (1994, 1973.) *Pedagogy of the oppressed.* Trans. Myra Bergman Ramos. New York: Continuum.

— (1990). *Education for critical consciousness.* New York: Continuum.

— (1990) and Myles Horton. *We make the road by walking: Conversations on education and social change.* Philadelphia: Temple University Press.

hooks, b. (2000). *Where we stand: Class matters.* New York: Routledge.

— (2000). *All about love: New visions.* New York: Harpers.

— (1994). *Teaching to transgress: Education as the practice of freedom.* New York, NY: Routledge.

Lorde, A. (1984). The transformation of silence into language and action. In *Sister Outsider* (pp. 40–44). New York, NY: Ten Speed Press.

Mipham, S. (2004). *Turning the mind into an ally.* New York, NY: Riverhead Books.

Nadal, K.L., Wong, W., Issa, M., Meterko, V., Leon, J., & Wideman, M. (2011). Sexual orientation microaggressions: Processes and coping mechanisms for lesbian, gay, and bisexual individuals. *Journal of LGBT Issues in Counseling, 5*, 21–46.

Oswald, R.F., Blume, L.B., & Marks, S.R. (2005). Decentering heteronormativity: A model for family studies. In V. L. Bengston (Ed.), *Sourcebook of Family Theory and Research* (pp. 143–165). Thousand Oaks, CA: Sage.

Palmer, P. (1998). *The courage to teach: Exploring the inner landscape of a teacher's life.* San Francisco, CA: Jossey-Bass.

Pinderhughes, E. (1989). *Race, ethnicity and power.* New York: The Free Press.

Sue, D. W. (2010). Microaggressions: More than just race. *Psychology Today.* https://www.psychologytoday.com/blog/microaggressions-in-everydaylife/201011/microaggressions-more-just-race.

Vaccaro, A., Annie Russell, E.I., & Koob, R.M. (2015). Students with minoritized identities of sexuality and gender in campus contexts: An emergent model. *New Directions for Student Services, 2015,* 152, 25–39.

Zinn, H. (1994). *You can't be neutral on a moving train: A personal history of our times.* Boston, MA: Beacon Press.

INDEX

creative tension, 249

crying, 156

curiosity, 192, 193

D

Daring Greatly: How the Courage to Be Vulnerable Transforms the Way We Live, Love, Parent, and Lead (Brown), 27

de-racialize, 135–136

developing intimacy, 71, 72

diaries. *See*, reflective diaries

Diffusing authority, 35

disagreement

    facilitators dealing with, 141-143

    microaggression vs., 131–138

discomfort, learning process and, 11–12

distractions, emotional explosions and, 175

Du Bois, W.E., 273

E

education system, 164

eggshell phenomena, 146–147

emotional explosions, 173–180

    distractions and, 175

    guiding principles and strategies, 180

    Instances of, 175

emotionally engaged research, 168–169

emotions, 153–162, 201

    anger. *See*, anger

    as gifts, 155. *as gifts* 156

    Chödrön, 160

crying, 154

fear, 158–159

feminist practice, 160, 162

managing, 156-157

value, 159-160

F

facilitators. *See also*, faculty of color

    authenticity and transparency, 149–150

    being neutral, 147, 148

    being objective, 139–152

    dealing with disareements, 141–143

    dealing with microaggression, 143–145

    guiding principles and strategies, 152

    neutralizing situation, 145–146

faculty of color

    assessment and grading of students, 145, 227–249

    consequences of raising racial issues, vi–11, 207–226

    guiding principles and strategies, 226

    Invisible Workload, 47–60

    opinions of, 209

    personal experience/stories, 103–111

    professional aspirations, 210

    responding to emotional explosions, 173–180

    responding to social issues in research and field work, 212, 213 responding to strong emotions in, 153–162

responding to tensions of 2016 presidential election, 181–203

self-care, 251–264

stress and fatigue, 208, 220

students evaluating, 214–215

unpacking, 212, 213

false humility, 33

fear, 158–159

feminist practice, 160, 162

field instructors, 167

field supervisors, 166, 168

field work, 163–171

    emotional engagement, 167

    guiding principles and strategies, 171

    instructors, 167, 168

    supervisors, 166

Fire Next Time (Baldwin), 253

Freire, Paulo, 13, 33, 41, 56, 82, 116, 246, 262, 271–272, 273

G

games, 259

give-and-take environment, 75–86

Goldman, Emma, 252

grade school, 121

H

handouts, 118

heteronormativity, 113

heterosexuals, 191–192

holding multiple truths, 188

homophobia, 41, 192

humanity, 37–38

hurt, 157–158

I

identity, 38

    anger and, 199

    sexual, 191–192

    shift, 106

    systemically marginalized, 45, 227, 264

institutional social capital, 53–54

intimacy, 71, 72, 75–86

    tried-and-true comrade, 82–85

intimate relationships, 34

Invisible Workload, 47–59

J

janitor, 259

Joseph, Barbara, 237

K

To Kill a Mockingbird, 186

L

laughing, 254

learning, 164

LGBTQ (lesbian, gay, bisexual, trans-gender, queer and, questioning), 10, 41–42

    faculty, dilemma regarding social issues, 207–226

    invisible workload, 47–60

    sexual identity development, 191–192

lived experience, 120

Living My Life (Goldman), 252

W

wholeheartedness, 27

Williams, Ovita, 168

willingness to be on the front lines,
83

Winnicott, Donald, 154

Y

Year of Yes (Rhimes), 258

Z

Zinn, Howard, 13–14, 148